Calling All Dogs!

Yoyo Yumyum Cubby Cupcake Doodle Dumpling Honey Kewpie Kibbles Muffin Nibbles Lampchop Lolly Poo Chubsy-ubsy Ciccia Crumpet Butterball Chiquita Boo Bobo Babykins Bebé Baby Amor Amoré Barne Shadow Sparky Murphy Sammy Roxy Zoe Sasha Angel Bonnie Abby Bailey Ginger Sophie Chlöe Lucy Lady Princess Sadie Daisy Maggie Molly Brandy Annie Katie Max Buddy Jake Sam Bailey Rocky Jessie Cody Bear Clyde Edgar Ernest Floyd Godfrey Grover Irving Harold Harvey Herma Agatha Agnes Bertha Betty Blanche Clovis Dinah Dorcas Doris Edit

Calling All Dogs!

Grrreat Names
for Your Perfect Pooch

Joanne O'Sullivan

LARK BOOKS
A Division of Sterling Publishing Co., Inc.
New York / London

DEVELOPMENT EDITOR:
Deborah Morgenthal

EDITOR:
Joanne O'Sullivan

ART DIRECTOR AND
ILLUSTRATOR:
Kristi Pfeffer

COVER DESIGNER:
Cindy LaBreacht

ASSOCIATE ART
DIRECTOR:
Shannon Yokeley

Library of Congress Cataloging-in-Publication Data

O'Sullivan, Joanne.
  Calling all dogs : grrreat [sic] names for your perfect pooch / Joanne
O'Sullivan. -- 1st ed.
      p. cm.
  ISBN-13: 978-1-60059-155-6 (pb-trade pbk. : alk. paper)
  ISBN-10: 1-60059-155-8 (pb-trade pbk. : alk. paper)
  1. Dogs--Names. I. Title.
  SF422.3.O88 2007
  636.7--dc22
                                        2007020822

10 9 8 7 6 5 4 3 2 1

First Edition

Published by Lark Books, A Division of
Sterling Publishing Co., Inc.
387 Park Avenue South, New York, N.Y. 10016

Text © 2007, Lark Books
Illustrations © 2007, Lark Books, unless otherwise specified

Distributed in Canada by Sterling Publishing,
c/o Canadian Manda Group, 165 Dufferin Street
Toronto, Ontario, Canada M6K 3H6

Distributed in the United Kingdom by GMC Distribution Services,
Castle Place, 166 High Street, Lewes, East Sussex, England BN7 1XU

Distributed in Australia by Capricorn Link (Australia) Pty Ltd.,
P.O. Box 704, Windsor, NSW 2756 Australia

If you have questions or comments about this book, please contact:
Lark Books
67 Broadway
Asheville, NC 28801
(828) 253-0467

Manufactured in China

ISBN-13: 978-1-60059-155-6
ISBN-10: 1-60059-155-8

For information about custom editions, special sales, premium and
corporate purchases, please contact Sterling Special Sales Department
at 800-805-5489 or specialsales@sterlingpub.com.

Contents

Introduction

In the past, choosing a dog name was easy: Fido, Spot, Rover—pick one and be done with it! But these days humans and dogs are on tighter terms: Our canine friends are not just there to retrieve ducks for us or round up the sheep. They are friends and companions—a part of the family. So selecting a name for your dog is more like the first step in a wonderful new relationship—one that will hopefully continue for many years. The sheer number of names available might seem overwhelming. Unlike the process of picking a name for a human child, you don't have to worry about family or cultural traditions. You're free to choose a name that reflects you, your dog, and his place in your family and in the world. This book will help you explore your options, organize your thinking, and help you select a name that's perfect for you and your dog.

HOW TO USE THIS BOOK

Dog names do not exist in a vacuum: Spend a little time getting to know your dog before choosing a name. Observe her personality, energy, style, and physical characteristics. Just like people, puppies and dogs have a certain *je ne sais quoi* that makes them complete individuals.

Now throw your personality and interests into the mix. What defines *you*? Your love of music, art, or history? Your amazing skill at video games? Your sense of humor? Your profession? Do you like the drama of a unique, attention-grabbing name or do you prefer something subtle and classic?

Look through the book. Some people are skimmers and scanners who flip through and find a name that just "feels" right. Others will methodically read every name, make lists and charts, and conduct informal polls of friends and relations to find the perfect match. Still others fall somewhere in between. Use the circles next to each name to check the ones you're interested in or to create a list, if you're that type. Or just try saying the names out loud.

Now you've got all the information you need to start matching a name to your pet. You might have decided that

The Shelf Life of Dog Names

If you're lucky, you're going to be living with your dog's name for up to 15 years. While it might be tempting to choose a name that's "ripped from the headlines" as they say, years from now you might find yourself scratching your head, wondering why on earth you chose a name whose 15 minutes of fame expired years ago. That's not to say that you can't choose something a bit trendy (see the Bow Wow Bling Bling section on page 101). But choose your cultural touchstones with a bit of discretion and lean toward names with something of a more lasting quality. There are plenty of dogs named Y2K still running around out there, which leaves a lot of people asking "Why?"

you will *definitely* name your dog after a musician. That's a good start, but is your dog a Dizzy, a Mozart, or a Lil' Bow Wow? That's where the chemistry of a good name kicks in: Assessing your dog's looks and personality will help you get the right fit.

Try calling the name out loud repeatedly (you can do this in the privacy of your own home if you feel silly doing it at the park). Call in different volumes and with different speeds. Does the name trip from the tongue or trip you up? This "test drive" can help you narrow down your options.

It might sound a little kooky, but ask your dog what she thinks. Try the name out with her and observe how she responds. If she doesn't react or looks away, you may have to try again. If she wags her tail and shows some energy, you may have a winner.

Never Underestimate the Power of Irony!

A mighty rottweiler named Duke; a toy fox terrier named Tiny—these are good names, no doubt about it—perfectly acceptable in every way. But if you want to move beyond acceptable into really memorable, consider the ironic twist: a black dog called Snowy, a white dog named Shadow, a tough guy named Princess, and little yappie dog named Rambo. When looking through names, in addition to the ones that suit your dog, consider ones that are quite the opposite of what's expected. You may find that you've hit upon the perfect foil for your canine companion.

CALL-ABILITY

For all practical purposes, your dog has a name for, well, practical purposes: so that she'll be able to recognize that you're talking to her and come when you call her. Dogs *do* have the ability to understand language—in fact, an average dog can understand up to 165 words. And the first and most important word he will learn is his name.

For this reason it's advisable to use a name that a puppy can easily recognize—three syllables max is a rule of thumb. More than that and your dog will lose interest and start to tune out (not unlike the famous *Far Side* cartoon that demonstrates what dogs *really* hear: "*blah, blah, blah,* **Ginger**, *blah blah blah.*"). Short and simple is a winning combination. That's not to say that you can't have your own special long, fancy name for your dog—Professor Henry Higgins, for example. But you will most certainly only use that "formal" name when making introductions for your dog. Most of the time he'll answer to just Henry.

Pedigree Names

If your dog has a pedigree, he already has a name. Breeders create names for all dogs born of their litters. These names are often quite long and fancy, including identifying details such as the strain of the breed, an identifying name for the litter, or the breeder or kennel's name. These names are registered with the kennel club of which the breeder is a member and are used when a dog is entered in a show. Because a pedigree name might be very long, such as Shadowsilk Dot Dot Dash at Holmelyne, pet owners often come up with a "call name" for a dog, which might be a shorter version of the long name (Shadow, for example, in this case) or a completely different name altogether. When you purchase your dog from the kennel, you'll receive a certificate of registration for the dog, which will include the dog's full name. You can keep the name or come up with a call name with more "call-ability."

Avoid names that sound like other commands: A dog may confuse "Joe" with "No" or have a hard time learning the "sit" command if his name is "Setter." Avoid using names similar to other members of the family: You don't want the dog to come running when you're calling your son to the dinner table.

Once you've chosen a name, try to use it consistently, at least when your dog is a pup. Trainers say that if a dog's name is used consistently before a command, the dog will learn skills much more easily. It's inevitable that you will end up creating variations on this name as time goes by (Sonny, Sonny Boy, Sonny Bo-Bo, etc.), but your dog should get used to his "call" name first. Try to use your dog's name whenever you want her; along with consistency, repetition is the key to communicating with your dog. When your dog is a pup, you may even want to add in a reward when she comes as called.

MY DOGGIE, MY SELF

Just as your choice of clothing or hairstyle tells the world a little something about you, your dog's name reflects your taste and personality. It is a "calling card" of sorts—you are going to be calling it, often at a very loud volume, in very public places. Statistics show that owners call their dogs more than 35,000 times in the dog's lifetime, so you really want a name that represents you in a favorable light.

While you shouldn't choose a dog name solely to impress people, the unavoidable fact is that humans, unlike dogs, do make judgments based on little more than a quick impression, or in this case, a name. While it's important to express your sense of humor, keep in mind that a name that's funny to your frat brothers may not fly well at the family reunion ("Grandma, I'd like you to meet Bong Hit..."), so unless you're really unconcerned with offending people, you might want to reserve such names as your special nicknames, rather than as your dog's real name. Likewise, you don't want to brand your dog as a biter or dangerous dog by giving it a name like Ripper: You don't *really* want him to live up to that.

Chances are that if you're reading this book, you're looking for a name with some meaning, some flair, something that reflects your interests or your world view. Make sure, for your sake and your dog's, to put your best face forward, and don't use your dog to make some kind of statement or point that you might not be comfortable with a few years from now.

Renaming Pound Puppies

You're at the pound, checking out all the adorable dogs available for adoption, trying to decide which one is right for you. There she is! That adorable little fluffy white mutt. You know that it was meant to be. There's only one problem: Her name is Peanut. You hate Peanuts. You're allergic to them—they make you swell up like a balloon. So what do you do? Move on to another pup, or turn Peanut into Princess? There are a few schools of thought on renaming adopted dogs. The first says: Don't do it. It's unfair to the dog and will lead to confusion—the dog will have no idea what name to answer to. The second says, feel free to rename as long as the dog is still a puppy. Puppies can adapt to a new name without too much difficulty, but more mature dogs are a little more stuck in their ways. A third way of thinking says that it's okay to change the name as long as it rhymes or is similar to the original name—Spot becomes Dot, Bingo is Ringo.

A final way of thinking, one that's gaining ground with trainers, is that it's perfectly fine to rename an adopted dog if a certain strategy is followed. Experts suggest combining the old and new name for a week or so. For example, if the dog's name is Duke and you want to change it to Daisy, call the dog by saying "Duke Daisy" for a while (putting emphasis on Daisy), and reward the dog when he comes. Gradually phase out the name Duke. Using positive reinforcement and associating rewards with the new name will help your dog learn, just as he learns other commands with these incentives.

If you don't know the dog's original name, start training her to use the name as you would train her to respond to other commands such as "sit" and "stay," that is, with positive reinforcement associated with her coming to you when called by that name.

Planet Poochie

It's a Dog's World

Sure, your dog may have come from the pound, but somewhere way back when, his ancestors came from somewhere else. Celebrate his fine breeding with a name chosen from his breed's country of origin (just a few of the hundreds of breeds and many countries in the world are listed here). Don't have a thoroughbred? Combine words from different countries or languages; wouldn't Bonjour Didgeridoo be a great name for a poodle/Australian terrier mix?

Australia

Australian Bulldog, Australian Cattle Dog, Australian Shepherd, Australian Kelpie, Australian Koolie, Australian Terrier

- Adelaide
- Aussie
- Barbie
- Billabong
- Boomerang
- Bushie
- Didgeridoo
- Dingo
- Dinkum
- Dinki-di
- Dundee
- Dreamtime
- Emu
- Jackaroo
- Jillaroo
- Kanga
- Koala
- Marmite
- Matilda
- Mate
- Sheila
- Sydney
- Wallaby
- Wallaroo
- Wombat

England

Beagle, Old English Bulldog, English Cocker Spaniel, English Foxhound, English Mastiff, English Pointer, English Setter, Old English Shepherd, English Springer Spaniel, English Terrier, Old English Sheepdog, Manchester Terrier

- ○ Ascot
- ○ Barking
- ○ Chester
- ○ Cricket
- ○ Devon
- ○ Dover
- ○ Empire
- ○ Eton
- ○ Hamish
- ○ Guvner
- ○ Harrod
- ○ Henley

- ○ Jack
- ○ Kipper
- ○ Monty
- ○ Nigel
- ○ Nigella
- ○ Pasty
- ○ Pip
- ○ Poppy
- ○ Posh
- ○ Pudding
- ○ Punt
- ○ Pym

- ○ Quid
- ○ Reginald
- ○ Robin Hood
- ○ Rugby
- ○ Rumpole
- ○ Snooker
- ○ Tuppance
- ○ Victoria
- ○ Wellie
- ○ Wembley
- ○ Wimbledon
- ○ Windsor

Denmark

Danish Broholmer, Danish Farm Dog, Great Dane

- ○ Blixen
- ○ Canute
- ○ Dagmar
- ○ Elkie
- ○ Ellsinore
- ○ Freja
- ○ Havarti

- ○ Hildegard
- ○ Lars
- ○ Olaf
- ○ Magnus
- ○ Marmaduke
- ○ Siegfried
- ○ Skat

- ○ Smuk
- ○ Sven
- ○ Tenna
- ○ Tilsit
- ○ Torben
- ○ Viggo
- ○ Vimse

France

Barbet, Basset Hound, Bichon Frisé (originally from Spain),
French Poodle, French Bulldog, French Brittany, French Spaniel

- Amélie
- Biarritz
- Bijoux
- Bisou
- Belle
- Cadaeu
- Cosette
- Délice
- Gallette
- Fifi
- Fleur
- Jacques
- Jeanne Marie
- Jolie
- Marcel
- Mon Ami
- Ma Chère
- Neige
- Petite Chou
- Pomme
- Soleil
- Solange
- Voilà

Germany

Boxer, Doberman, German Shepard, German Pointer, German
Spaniel, German Spitz, German Pinscher, Weimeraner

- Alpen
- Bärchen
- Bitte
- Bruno
- Fräulein
- Freund
- Fritz
- Gerhard
- Greta
- Gretel
- Gunner
- Günter
- Hoenig
- Knuddel
- Klaus
- Liebling
- Ludwig
- Otto
- Schatzi
- Schnitzel
- Rolf
- Spatzi
- Strudel
- Waldo
- Wolfgang

Ireland

Irish Bull Terrier, Irish Setter, Irish Wolfhound, Kerry Blue Terrier. Kerry Beagle, Irish Water Spaniel

- Blarney
- Bridget
- Casey
- Clancy
- Danny Boy
- Dingle
- Duffy
- Dublin
- Fergal

- Fergus
- Finnegan
- Galway
- Guinness
- Kerry
- Kilkenny
- Murphy
- O'Malley

- Paddy
- Reilly
- Rooney
- Seamus
- Shannon
- Sweeney
- Tipperary
- Yeats

Italy

Bergamesco, Bracco Italiano, Italian Greyhound, Lagotto Romagnolo

- Aldo
- Amoré
- Avanti
- Bambina (o)
- Bella (o)
- Bimba (o)
- Ciao
- Ciro
- Dante
- Dario

- Enzo
- Fabio
- Fabrizio
- Giorgio
- Giacomo
- Guido
- Maestro
- Mona Lisa
- Napoli
- Pazzo

- Piccolo
- Pisa
- Primo
- Pronto
- Prego
- Puccini
- Primo
- Strega

Note: a endings for female; o endings for male

Japan

Akita, Japanese Chin, Japanese Mastiff, Japanese Spitz, Japanese Terrier

- Chibi
- Fuji
- Jiro
- Kiku
- Kokoro
- Kyoto
- Miso

- Mochi
- Momo
- Ringo
- Saki
- Sakura
- Sashimi
- Soba

- Sushi
- Taro
- Tempe
- Udon
- Wasabi
- Yuuki
- Yumi

Mexico

Chihuahua, Mexican Hairless

- Amigo
- Amiga
- Amor
- Bandito
- Bolero
- Bianca
- Chica (o)
- Chiquita
- Corazon

- Enchilada
- Estrella
- Fajita
- Lobo
- Luna
- Lupe
- Mariachi
- Mole

- Nacho
- Niña (o)
- Pancho
- Pepe
- Pepita
- Paco
- Rosita
- Salsa

Note: a endings for female; o endings for male

Russia

Borzoi, Russian Black Terrier, Russian Harlequin Hound, Russian Spaniel, Russian Wolfhound, Russian Toy Terrier, Siberian Husky

- Alexei
- Boris
- Borscht
- Chekov
- Dmitri
- Fyodor
- Ily
- Ivan
- Kiev
- Kremlin
- Mischa
- Nicolai
- Olga
- Pavel
- Nikita
- Sasha
- Sergei
- Svetlana
- Tatiana
- Vladimir
- Valery
- Vasily
- Vladimir
- Yevgeny

Scotland

Cairn Terrier, Scottish Deerhound, Scottish Terrier, West Highland Terrier, Skye Terrier, Shetland Sheepdog

- Argyle
- Angus
- Bonnie
- Bruce
- Burns
- Dewar
- Duff
- Duncan
- Dumfrie
- Dundee
- Ewan
- Haggis
- Heather
- Highlander
- Hume
- Kiltie
- Lachlan
- MacIntosh
- McDougal
- McDuff
- McGregor
- McKenzie
- Nessie
- Orkney
- Plaid
- Stewart
- Tam O' Shanter
- Tartan

Spain

Spanish Greyhound, Spanish Mastiff, Spanish Water Dog

- ○ Azul
- ○ Bianca
- ○ Bonita
- ○ Consuela
- ○ Corazon
- ○ Esmeralda
- ○ Esperanza
- ○ Fernando
- ○ Flamenca (o)
- ○ Gitano
- ○ Ibiza
- ○ Inez
- ○ Inigo
- ○ Luz
- ○ Paloma
- ○ Pilar
- ○ Paz
- ○ Placida (o)
- ○ Ramon
- ○ Rico
- ○ Sangria
- ○ Tapas
- ○ Toro

Note: a endings for female; o endings for male

Sweden

Swedish Elkhound, Swedish Lapphund, Swedish Valhund

- ○ Annika
- ○ Astrid
- ○ Björn
- ○ Britta
- ○ Frida
- ○ Greta
- ○ Gudren
- ○ Gunnar
- ○ Gunilla
- ○ Hedda
- ○ Inge
- ○ Ingeborg
- ○ Ingmar
- ○ Jens
- ○ Lars
- ○ Leif
- ○ Pellé
- ○ Pernilla
- ○ Sonja
- ○ Søren
- ○ Stefan
- ○ Stellan
- ○ Sven

Tibet

Lhasa Apso, Tibetan Mastiff, Tibetan Spaniel, Tibetan Terrier

- Daku
- Danu
- Diki
- Gurmi
- Jangbu
- Jangmu
- Kibi

- Kitsi
- Lobsang
- Rinche
- Norbu
- Pemba
- Phuti
- Sherpa
- Tashi

- Tenzen
- Tenzing
- Tuchi
- Tuli
- Tutu
- Yangji
- Zopa

Wales

Welsh Corgi, Cardigan Welsh Corgi, Pembroke Welsh Corgi, Welsh Springer Spaniel, Welsh Terrier

- Bangor
- Bran
- Bryn
- Carys
- Cerridwyn
- Dilys

- Dylan
- Glynis
- Llewellyn
- Lloyd
- Llyr
- Madog

- Morgen
- Rhiannon
- Rhys
- Snowdon
- Swansea
- Twyn

A Walk Around The Block

Did you leave your heart in 'Frisco? Is Georgia always on your mind? You might choose a name that reminds you of home or of your favorite destination. Or you might just choose a place name that fits your dog's personality: A flashy dog with star quality would happily answer to the name Hollywood. A rough-and-tumble macho dog may call to mind a cowboy name like Dakota.

- Alamo
- Aspen
- Aruba
- Aussie
- Bahama
- Bali
- Baja
- Bayou
- Boca
- Broadway
- Brooklyn
- Carolina
- Carmel
- Casbah
- Catalina

- Cayman
- Catalina
- Cheyenne
- Chilliwack
- Congo
- Cortez
- Cuba
- Dallas
- Dakota
- Danube
- D.C.
- Delhi
- Dixie
- Djibouti
- Dublin

- Durango
- Fez
- Fiji
- Fuji
- Frisco
- Galway
- Georgia
- Hollywood
- India
- Jamaica
- Jersey
- Kenya
- Kerry
- Klondike
- Kodiak

- ○ Kona
- ○ Kyoto
- ○ Laredo
- ○ Lhasa
- ○ Panama
- ○ Philly
- ○ Malibu
- ○ Maui
- ○ Milan
- ○ Monterrey
- ○ Mumbai
- ○ Napa
- ○ Niagara
- ○ Oaxaca
- ○ Odessa

- ○ Oahu
- ○ Orlando
- ○ Paris
- ○ Portobello
- ○ Phuket
- ○ Rebel
- ○ Reno
- ○ Rio
- ○ Roma
- ○ Santiago
- ○ Savannah
- ○ Sedona
- ○ Siena
- ○ Sligo
- ○ Sitka
- ○ Sonora

- ○ Sydney
- ○ Taos
- ○ Tahoe
- ○ Tex
- ○ Thames
- ○ Tijuana
- ○ Timbuktu
- ○ Togo
- ○ Toulouse
- ○ Surrey
- ○ Vegas
- ○ Woodstock
- ○ Yankee
- ○ Yukon
- ○ Zanzibar

Out of This World

Why stop at the upper edges of the atmosphere when picking your dog's name? A planet name or celestial-sounding name is a strong choice that's unusual without being outlandish. Unless you want to be outlandish. In that case, you might choose a place that exists only in legend or between the pages of a book. The names of fantasy lands or cities are often delightfully lyrical and fun to say out loud. Imagine yourself at the dog park calling "Rivendell! Rivendell!" You're sure to attract the attention of not only your dog, but some like-minded fantasy fans as well.

- Alegaësia
- Andromeda
- Arcadia
- Atlantis
- Avalon
- Camelot
- Cassiopeia
- Earthsea
- Eden
- El Dorado
- Endor
- Fantastica
- Gwynedd
- Heaven
- Halle-Bopp
- Hogwarts
- Jupiter
- Kelewan
- Mars
- Mercury
- Mystara
- Narnia
- Neptune
- Orion
- Oz
- Pluto
- Polaris
- Rivendell
- Saturn
- Shangri-la
- Tara
- Venus
- Westeros

Make It Personal

Think about places that mean something to you. If you've moved around a lot you may want to choose the name of the place you were born, or the name of the street on which you grew up. Or how about the name of the place you went on your first date with your partner? Of course you don't want to call your dog "Regal Cinema 14," but if you happened to have gone to a cute bistro called Mario's Café, it could be a meaningful choice that brings up pleasant memories.

Stars of Stage and Screen

Small Screen Dogs

Dogs have always had an important role to play on television. What would Frasier have been without Eddie? Consider a TV dog name, or choose the name of a memorable human character—one whose name you don't mind repeating again and again each day.

NAME	SHOW
○ Ace	*Batman*
○ Alpha Dog	*Bewitched*
○ August	*American Chopper*
○ Backup	*Veronica Mars*
○ Benji	*Benji*
○ Brandon the Wonder Dog	*Punky Brewster*
○ Boomer	*Here's Boomer*
○ Bouncer	*Neighbours*
○ Buddy	*Veronica's Closet*
○ Bullet the Wonder Dog	*The Roy Rogers Show*
○ Charlie the Wonder Dog	*The Late Show*

NAME	SHOW
○ Chester	*The Nanny*
○ Claude	*The Beverly Hillbillies*
○ Comet	*Full House*
○ Cynthia	*Green Acres*
○ Dreyfus	*Empty Nest*
○ Duke	*The Beverly Hillbillies*
○ Eddie	*Frasier*
○ Elizabeth Taylor	*Sex and the City*
○ Fang	*Columbo*
○ Freeway	*Hart to Hart*
○ Flash	*The Dukes of Hazzard*
○ Fred	*I Love Lucy*
○ Happy	*7th Heaven*
○ Lassie	*Lassie*
○ Maximillion	*The Bionic Woman*
○ Mignon	*Green Acres*
○ Murray	*Mad About You*
○ Nancy	*Unfabulous*
○ Paul Anka	*Gilmore Girls*
○ Pete the Pup	*Our Gang*
○ Porthos	*Star Trek: Enterprise*
○ Princess Dandyridge Brandywine	*Sex and the City*
○ Queegqueg	*The X-Files*
○ Sedge	*Stargate: Atlantis*
○ Stinky and Nunzio	*Dharma and Greg*
○ Sugar	*The X-Files*
○ Tiger	*The Brady Bunch*
○ Triumph, the Insult Comic Dog	*Late Night with Conan O'Brien*

NAME	SHOW
⭕ Truffles	*George & Mildred*
⭕ Vincent	*Lost*
⭕ Wellard	*EastEnders*
⭕ Wildmutt	*Ben 10*
⭕ Wishbone	*Wishbone*
⭕ Wubbie	*The Andy Milonakis Show*
⭕ Zeus and Apollo	*Magnum, P.I.*

TV Characters That Aren't Dogs

NAME	SHOW
○ Alfalfa	*Our Gang*
○ Beeker	*The Muppet Show*
○ Bones	*Star Trek*
○ Buffy	*Buffy the Vampire Slayer*
○ Captain Kirk	*Star Trek*
○ Columbo	*Columbo*
○ Costanza	*Seinfeld*
○ Elmo	*Sesame Street*
○ Frasier	*Frasier*
○ Gilligan	*Gillian's Island*
○ Gomer	*Gomer Pyle*
○ Gomez	*The Addams Family*
○ Gonzo	*The Muppet Show*
○ Goober	*Gomer Pyle*
○ Fonzi	*Happy Days*
○ Hawkeye	*M*A*S*H*
○ Hot Lips	*M*A*S*H*
○ Kermit	*The Muppet Show*
○ Lurch	*The Addams Family*
○ Monk	*Monk*
○ Morticia	*The Addams Family*
○ Mulder	*The X-Files*
○ Opie	*The Andy Griffith Show*
○ Scully	*The X-Files*
○ Spock	*Star Trek*
○ Tonto	*The Lone Ranger*
○ Urke	*Family Matters*
○ Xena	*Xena: Warrior Princess*

Big Screen Dogs

Can you imagine Turner without Hooch? If your very own canine co-star reminds you of one of these Hollywood legends, why not name him in the dog star's honor?

NAME	MOVIE
○ Andrew	*Mary Poppins*
○ Bailey	*Bailey's Billions*
○ Baxter	*Anchorman: The Legend of Ron Burgundy*
○ Beethoven	*Beethoven*
○ Benji	*Benji*
○ Bernie	*Meet the Fockers*
○ Big Red	*Big Red*
○ Blood	*A Boy and His Dog*
○ Bruiser	*Legally Blonde*
○ Butkus	*Rocky*
○ Buckley	*The Royal Tenenbaums*
○ Buddy	*Air Bud*
○ Chance	*Homeward Bound*
○ Cody	*The Life Aquatic with Steve Zissou*
○ Copernicus	*Back to the Future*
○ Dog	*Big Jake, Mad Max 2*
○ Einstein	*Back to the Future*
○ Fly	*Babe*
○ Frank	*Men in Black*
○ Fred	*Smokey and the Bandit*

NAME	MOVIE
○ Gort	*There's Something About Mary*
○ Grunt	*Flashdance*
○ Hubble	*Good Boy!*
○ Harvey	*E.T.*
○ Hercules	*The Sandlot*
○ Hooch	*Turner and Hooch*
○ Hoser	*Strange Brew*
○ Jerry Lee	*K-9*
○ Kerouac	*Down and Out in Beverly Hills*
○ Lucky	*Homeward Bound*
○ Matisse	*Down and Out in Beverly Hills*
○ Michelangelo	*Beethoven's 4th*
○ Milo	*The Mask*
○ Missy	*Beethoven's 2nd*
○ Moses	*Dogville, Meet the Fockers*
○ Mr. Beefy	*Little Nicky*
○ Nanook	*The Lost Boys*
○ Nikki	*Nikki, The Wild Dog of the North*
○ Old Yeller	*Old Yeller*
○ Otis	*Milo and Otis*
○ Odie	*Garfield*
○ Pac-Man	*Blade: Trinity*
○ Precious	*Silence of the Lambs*

NAME	MOVIE
◯ Roz	*Meet the Fockers*
◯ Sandy	*Annie*
◯ Shadow	*Homeward Bound*
◯ Skip	*My Dog Skip*
◯ Sparky	*Michael*
◯ Strongheart	*Strongheart*
◯ Tango	*Tango and Cash*
◯ Toto	*The Wizard of Oz*
◯ Verdell	*As Good As It Gets*

Movie Characters That Aren't Dogs

NAME	MOVIE
◯ Alfie	*Alfie*
◯ Bond	*James Bond* movies
◯ Captain Jack	*Pirates of the Caribbean*
◯ Dirty Harry	*Dirty Harry*
◯ E.T.	*E.T.*
◯ Gidget	*Gidget*
◯ Foxy Brown	*Foxy Brown*
◯ Han Solo	*Star Wars*
◯ Indiana Jones	*Indiana Jones* movies
◯ M	*James Bond* movies
◯ McFly	*Back to the Future*
◯ Miss Moneypenny	*James Bond* movies
◯ Morpheus	*The Matrix*
◯ Neo	*The Matrix*
◯ Obi-Wan	*Star Wars*
◯ Princess Leia	*Star Wars*

NAME	MOVIE
◯ Q	*James Bond* movies
◯ Rhett	*Gone with the Wind*
◯ Rocky	*Rocky*
◯ Sam Spade	*The Maltese Falcon*
◯ Scarface	*Scarface*
◯ Scarlett	*Gone with the Wind*
◯ Shaft	*Shaft*
◯ Spartacus	*Spartacus*
◯ Spicoli	*Fast Times at Ridgemont High*
◯ Sundance	*Butch Cassidy and the Sundance Kid*
◯ Trinity	*The Matrix*
◯ Yoda	*Star Wars*
◯ Zorro	*The Mask of Zorro*

By the Book
Between the Pages

Your dog may chew covers and eat pages, but you can be both a dog lover and a book lover. Between the pages of your favorite books are tons of great character names, some of which are given to dogs, others to humans or imaginary creatures. Classic legends, fairy tales, and children's stories are other great sources for unforgettable names.

NAME	BOOK
○ Ahab	*Moby Dick*
○ Aladdin	*Arabian Nights*
○ Artful Dodger	*Oliver Twist*
○ Aslan	*The Chronicles of Narnia*
○ Atticus	*To Kill a Mockingbird*
○ Bartleby	*Bartleby, the Scrivener*
○ Bilbo Baggins	*The Hobbit*
○ Beowulf	*Beowulf*
○ Crusoe	*Robinson Crusoe*
○ Cyrano	*Cyrano de Bergerac*
○ Dulcinea	*Don Quixote*
○ Dumbledore	*Harry Potter*
○ Eeyore	*Winnie the Pooh*
○ Fagin	*Oliver Twist*

NAME	BOOK
○ Faust	*Dr. Faustus*
○ Frodo	*Lord of the Rings*
○ Gandalf	*Lord of the Rings*
○ Garp	*The World According to Garp*
○ Gatsby	*The Great Gatsby*
○ Gawain	*Le Morte D'Arthur*
○ Gretel	*Hansel and Gretel*
○ Guinevere	*Le Morte D'Arthur*
○ Goldilocks	*Goldilocks and the Three Bears*
○ Grawp	*Harry Potter*
○ Grendel	*Beowulf*
○ Gulliver	*Gulliver's Travels*
○ Hagrid	*Harry Potter*
○ Hermione	*Harry Potter*
○ Hansel	*Hansel and Gretel*
○ Heathcliff	*Wuthering Heights*
○ Heidi	*Heidi*
○ Holden	*The Catcher in the Rye*
○ Horton	*Horton Hears a Who*

NAME	BOOK
◯ Huck	*Huckleberry Finn*
◯ Jeeves	*Jeeves* books
◯ Lancelot	*Le Morte D'Arthur*
◯ Lolita	*Lolita*
◯ Lorax	*The Lorax*
◯ Marley	*A Christmas Carol*
◯ Merlin	*Le Morte D'Arthur*
◯ Miss Havisham	*Great Expectations*
◯ Moll Flanders	*Moll Flanders*
◯ Meaursault	*The Stranger*
◯ Oliver Twist	*Oliver Twist*
◯ Peter Pan	*Peter Pan*
◯ Peeves	*Harry Potter*
◯ Pip	*Great Expectations*
◯ Pippi	*The New Adventures of Pippi Longstocking*
◯ Puddleglum	*The Chronicles of Narnia*
◯ Robin Hood	*Robin Hood*
◯ Rumpelstiltskin	*Rumpelstiltskin*
◯ Rapunzel	*Rapunzel*
◯ Mowgli	*The Jungle Book*
◯ Mr. Darcy	*Pride and Prejudice*
◯ Scrooge	*A Christmas Carol*
◯ Sherlock	*Sherlock Holmes*
◯ Scheherazade	*Arabian Nights*
◯ Sinbad	*Arabian Nights*
◯ Sir Percival	*Le Morte D'Arthur*
◯ Scout	*To Kill a Mockingbird*
◯ Sula	*Sula*
◯ Tigger	*Winnie the Pooh*

NAME	BOOK
○ Tiny Tim	*A Christmas Carol*
○ Tonks	*Harry Potter*
○ Tumnus	*The Chronicles of Narnia*
○ Quixote	*Don Quixote*
○ Wonka	*Willy Wonka and the Chocolate Factory*
○ Wilbur	*Charlotte's Web*

Thou Call'dst Me Dog

It's tough to top the Bard: Who can forget names like Puck, Iago, and Caliban? It's that instant name recognition that makes these monikers so memorable.

NAME	PLAY
○ Alonso	*The Tempest*
○ Ariel	*The Tempest*
○ Bagot	*Richard II*
○ Balthasar	*Much Ado About Nothing*

NAME	PLAY
○ Banquo	*Macbeth*
○ Bassanio	*Merchant of Venice*
○ Benvolio	*Romeo and Juliet*
○ Bianca	*The Taming of the Shrew*
○ Blondello	*The Taming of the Shrew*
○ Borachio	*Much Ado About Nothing*
○ Caliban	*The Tempest*
○ Cadwal	*Cymbeline*
○ Catesby	*Richard III*
○ Celia	*As You Like It*
○ Cicero	*Julius Caesar*
○ Claudio	*Much Ado About Nothing*
○ Cordelia	*King Lear*
○ Corin	*As You Like It*
○ Desdemona	*Othello*
○ Dogberry	*Much Ado About Nothing*
○ Dromio	*A Comedy of Errors*
○ Falstaff	*Henry IV*
○ Flavius	*Timon of Athens*

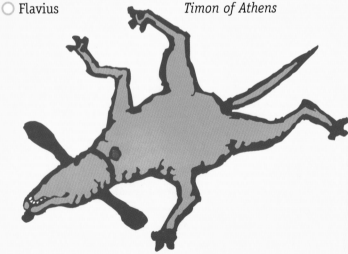

NAME	PLAY
○ Florizel	*The Winter's Tale*
○ Froth	*Measure for Measure*
○ Gadshill	*Henry IV*
○ Gonzalo	*The Tempest*
○ Grumio	*The Taming of the Shrew*
○ Guildenstern	*Hamlet*
○ Hamlet	*Hamlet*
○ Hecate	*Macbeth*
○ Hermia	*A Midsummer Night's Dream*
○ Hotspur	*Henry IV*
○ Iago	*Othello*
○ Lord Scroop	*Henry V*
○ Jachimo	*Cymbeline*
○ Juliet	*Romeo and Juliet*
○ Laertes	*Hamlet*
○ Lysander	*A Midsummer Night's Dream*
○ Macbeth	*Macbeth*
○ Macduff	*Macbeth*
○ Malvolio	*Twelfth Night*
○ Mistress Quickly	*The Merry Wives of Windsor*
○ Monsieur LeBeau	*As You Like It*
○ Mopsa	*The Winter's Tale*
○ Mote	*Love's Labour's Lost*

NAME	PLAY
○ Moth	*A Midsummer Night's Dream*
○ Nym	*Merry Wives of Windsor*
○ Oberon	*A Midsummer Night's Dream*
○ Ophelia	*Hamlet*
○ Orsino	*Twelfth Night*
○ Othello	*Othello*
○ Orlando	*As You Like It*
○ Peaseblossom	*A Midsummer Night's Dream*
○ Perdita	*The Winter's Tale*
○ Portia	*Merchant of Venice*
○ Puck	*A Midsummer Night's Dream*
○ Prospero	*The Tempest*
○ Romeo	*Romeo and Juliet*
○ Rosencranz	*Hamlet*
○ Tatiana	*A Midsummer Night's Dream*
○ Yorick	*Hamlet*

A Dog's Tale

A dog is often the star of the story in her own right. Here are the names of some literary hounds:

NAME	STORY
◯ Argos	*The Odyssey*
◯ Asta	*The Thin Man*
◯ Banga	*The Master and Margarita*
◯ Beautiful Joe	*Beautiful Joe*
◯ Barnabus	*The Sandman*
◯ Big Red	*Big Red and Other Stories*
◯ Bluebell	*Animal Farm*
◯ Boatswain	*Typee*
◯ Bodger	*The Incredible Journey*
◯ Boots	*Thy Servant a Dog*
◯ Buck	*Call of the Wild*
◯ Bullseye	*Oliver Twist*
◯ Cavall	*King Arthur's Dog*
◯ Desmond	*Vineland*
◯ Dingo	*A Captain at Fifteen*
◯ Enrique	*Tortilla Flat*
◯ Fairy Wogdog	*Watership Down*
◯ Fluffy	*Harry Potter and the Sorcerer's Stone*
◯ Duchess	*The Pie and the Patty Pan*
◯ Einstein	*Watchers*
◯ Fang	*Mason & Dixon*
◯ Ginger Pye	*Ginger Pye*

NAME	STORY
⭘ Garm	*Farmer Giles of Ham*
⭘ Jip	*Doctor Dolittle, David Copperfield*
⭘ Kep	*The Tale of Jemima Puddle-Duck*
⭘ Kipper	*Kipper the Dog*
⭘ Kashtanka	*Kashtanka*
⭘ Little Ann	*Where the Red Fern Grows*
⭘ Lad	*Lad: A Dog*
⭘ Leo	*Dogsbody*
⭘ Lorelei	*The Dogs of Babel*
⭘ Marley	*Marley and Me*
⭘ Montmorency	*Three Men in a Boat: To Say Nothing of the Dog!*
⭘ Old Dan	*Where the Red Fern Grows*
⭘ Padfoot	*Harry Potter*
⭘ Patrasche	*A Dog of Flanders*
⭘ Pickles	*Ginger and Pickles*
⭘ Pilot	*Jane Eyre*
⭘ Ponch	*Young Wizards*
⭘ Pugnax	*Against the Day*
⭘ Rigsby	*Henry Huggins*
⭘ Rowf	*Plague Dogs*

NAME	STORY
○ Huan	*The Silmarillion*
○ Nero	*Little House: The First Years*
○ Shiloh	*Shiloh*
○ Scupper	*The Sailor Dog*
○ Snitter	*Plague Dogs*
○ Sounder	*Sounder*
○ Toby	*The Sign of Four*
○ Togo	*Nancy Drew* books
○ Wellington	*The Curious Incident of the Dog in the Night-time*
○ White Fang	*White Fang*
○ Winn Dixie	*Because of Winn Dixie*

See You in the Funny Pages

woof!

Cartoon Dogs

Wouldn't it be great if real dogs could be like cartoon dogs? They'd be able to talk, have superpowers, and come in all different colors from magenta to sea-foam green. Some of these amazing creatures—found in animé, cartoons, comic strips, and animated films—also have amazing names. Is one of them right for your superpup?

NAME	CARTOON
○ Ace, The Bat-Hound	*Batman*
○ Alexander	*FullMetal Alchemist*
○ Astro	*The Jetsons*
○ Augie Doggie	*The Quick Draw McGraw Show*
○ Doggie Daddy	*The Quick Draw McGraw Show*
○ Baby Cinnamon	*Hello Kitty*
○ Bandit	*Jonny Quest*
○ Barkley	*Sesame Street*
○ Beauregard	*Pogo*
○ Beekay (B.K.)	*Freefall*
○ Belle	*Belle et Sébastien*
○ Blue and Magenta	*Blue's Clues*

NAME	CARTOON
⚪ Brain	*Inspector Gadget*
⚪ Brian Griffin	*Family Guy*
⚪ Burp	*Gerald McBoing Boing*
⚪ Buttons	*Animaniacs*
⚪ CatDog	*Catdog*
⚪ Checkers Hibiki	*Ranma ½*
⚪ Clifford	*Clifford The Big Red Dog*
⚪ Daisy	*Blondie*
⚪ Den	*FullMetal Alchemist*
⚪ Dino	*The Flintstones*
⚪ Dinsdale	*Rubbish, King of the Jumble*
⚪ Dogbert	*Dilbert*
⚪ Dogfather	*The Dogfather*
⚪ Doggy	*King of the Hill*
⚪ Dogmatix	*Asterix*
⚪ Doidle	*The Fairly OddParents*
⚪ Dollar	*Richie Rich*
⚪ Doogal	*Doogal*
⚪ Dynomutt, Dog Wonder	*Dynomutt*
⚪ Edward	*MÄR*
⚪ Ein	*Cowboy Bebop*
⚪ Elektra	*Cathy*
⚪ Goliath	*Davey and Goliath*
⚪ Goddard	*Jimmy Neutron: Boy Genius*
⚪ Grimm	*Mother Goose and Grimm*
⚪ Gromit	*Wallace and Gromit*
⚪ Hotdog	*Archie*
⚪ Hector	*Looney Toons*

NAME	CARTOON
◯ Hong Kong Phooey	*Hanna-Barbera cartoon*
◯ Huckleberry Hound	*Hanna-Barbera cartoon*
◯ Idéfix	*Asterix*
◯ Jasper	*Family Guy*
◯ Koji	*Zetsuai 1989*
◯ Krypto	*Superman*
◯ Laddie	*The Simpsons*
◯ Ladybird	*King of the Hill*
◯ Little Monty	*The Simpsons*
◯ Loyal Heart Dog	*Care Bears*
◯ Marc Antony	*Loony Toons*
◯ Marmaduke	*Marmaduke*
◯ Max	*How The Grinch Stole Christmas!*
◯ Mr. Peabody	*The Rocky and Bullwinkle Show*
◯ Ms. Lion	*Spider-Man and his Amazing Friends*
◯ Mulch	*Groo the Wanderer*
◯ Otto	*Beetle Bailey*
◯ Pal	*Arthur*
◯ Pero	*Astro Boy*
◯ Pochacco	*Hello Kitty*
◯ Poochie	*The Simpsons*
◯ Poochini	*Poochini*
◯ Pooka	*Anastasia*
◯ Porkchop	*Doug*
◯ Preston	*Wallace and Gromit*
◯ Rin Tin Tin	*The Adventures of Rex and Rinty*

NAME	CARTOON
⭘ Rowlf	*The Muppet Show*
⭘ Ren Höek	*Ren and Stimpy*
⭘ Runt	*Animaniacs*
⭘ Santa's Little Helper	*The Simpsons*
⭘ Satchel Pooch	*Get Fuzzy*
⭘ Scooby-Doo	*Scooby-Doo*
⭘ Scooby-Dum	*Scooby-Doo*
⭘ Scrappy-Doo	*Scooby-Doo*
⭘ Sharky the Sharkdog	*Eek! the Cat*
⭘ Snert	*Hagar the Horrible*
⭘ Snoopy	*Peanuts*
⭘ Snowy	*The Adventures of Tintin*
⭘ Sophie	*Dog Eat Doug*
⭘ Sparky	*South Park*
⭘ Spike	*Rugrats*
⭘ Sprocket	*Fraggle Rock*
⭘ Spunky	*Rocko's Modern Life*
⭘ Stu	*Littlest Pet Shop*
⭘ Tyke	*Tom and Jerry*
⭘ Underdog	*Underdog*
⭘ Wolfram Blitzen	*Newshounds*
⭘ Yakko, Wakko, and Dot	*Animaniacs*
⭘ Zero	*The Nightmare Before Christmas*

Disney Dogs

NAME	MOVIE OR TV SHOW
○ Angel	*Lady and the Tramp II*
○ Balto	*Balto*
○ Boliver	*Mickey Mouse*
○ Brandy	*Brandy and Mr. Whiskers*
○ Bruno	*Cinderella*
○ Charlie	*All Dogs Go to Heaven*
○ Chief	*Fox and the Hound*
○ Cooper	*Fox and the Hound*
○ Dodger	*Oliver and Company*
○ Dr. Doppler	*Treasure Planet*
○ Fifi the Peke	*Mickey Mouse*
○ Fu Dog	*American Dragon: Jake Long*
○ Goofy	*Mickey Mouse*
○ Lady	*Lady and the Tramp*
○ Lafayette	*The Aristocats*
○ Little Brother	*Mulan*
○ Jock	*Lady and the Tramp*
○ Napoleon	*The Aristocats*
○ Oliver	*Oliver and Company*
○ Peg	*Lady and the Tramp*
○ Percy	*Pocahontas*
○ Pluto	*Mickey Mouse*
○ Pongo	*101 Dalmatians*
○ Perdita	*101 Dalmatians*
○ Lucky	*101 Dalmatians*
○ Rolly	*101 Dalmatians*
○ Scamp	*Lady and the Tramp*
○ Slinky	*Toy Story*
○ Tramp	*Lady and the Tramp*
○ Trusty	*Lady and the Tramp*

Other Cartoon Inspirations

Don't limit yourself to dogs when scouring the cartoon universe for a name. What about a cat's name? A turtle? A mermaid? Check out some of these animated aliases.

NAME	INSPIRATION
◯ Ariel	*The Little Mermaid*
◯ Bam Bam	*The Flintstones*
◯ Bambi	*Bambi*
◯ Bart	*The Simpsons*
◯ Batfink	*Boomerang*
◯ Belle	*Beauty and the Beast*
◯ Bluto	*Popeye*
◯ Bullwinkle	*The Rocky and Bullwinkle Show*
◯ Buzz	*Toy Story*
◯ Charlie Brown	*Peanuts*
◯ Cinderella	*Cinderella*
◯ Crush	*Finding Nemo*
◯ Dory	*Finding Nemo*
◯ Dumbo	*Dumbo*
◯ Goldeen	*Pokemon*
◯ Grumpy	*Snow White and the Seven Dwarfs*
◯ Gumby	*Gumby*

NAME	INSPIRATION
◯ Homer	*The Simpsons*
◯ Itchy	*The Simpsons*
◯ Jiminy Cricket	*Pinocchio*
◯ Kanga	*Winnie the Pooh*
◯ Lilo	*Lilo and Stitch*
◯ Linus	*Peanuts*
◯ Lumière	*Beauty and the Beast*
◯ Marlin	*Finding Nemo*
◯ Marge	*The Simpsons*
◯ Marty	*Madagascar*
◯ Melman	*Madagascar*
◯ Mulan	*Mulan*
◯ Mu-shu	*Mulan*
◯ Nala	*The Lion King*
◯ Nemo	*Finding Nemo*
◯ Pebbles	*The Flintstones*
◯ Pepé le Pew	*Loony Tunes*
◯ Pinocchico	*Pinocchio*
◯ Paddington	*Paddington Bear*
◯ Pikachu	*Pokeman*
◯ Pogo	*Pogo*
◯ Popeye	*Popeye*
◯ Pumbaa	*The Lion King*
◯ Sluggo	*Nancy*
◯ Sandy Cheeks	*SpongeBob SquarePants*
◯ Scratchy	*The Simpsons*
◯ Simba	*The Lion King*

NAME	INSPIRATION
○ Sleepy	*Snow White and the Seven Dwarfs*
○ Snuffy	*Popeye*
○ Speedy Gonzalez	*Looney Tunes*
○ Sponge Bob	*SpongeBob SquarePants*
○ Stitch	*Lilo and Stitch*
○ Tarzan	*Tarzan*
○ Taz	*Looney Tunes*
○ Thumper	*Bambi*
○ Tinker Bell	*Peter Pan*
○ Tigger	*Winnie the Pooh*
○ Timon	*The Lion King*
○ Tosky	*Aquaman*
○ Tweety	*Looney Tunes*
○ Wile E. Coyote	*Road Runner*
○ Wimpie	*Popeye*
○ Yogi	*Yogi Bear*

Yes, Sir, That's My Baby

The hottest dog names now are those you're just as likely to hear on the playground as at the dog park. Today's trend toward human names for dogs reflects dogs' up-and-coming status. No longer just a pet, a dog is part of the family, and choosing a name for one involves the kind of forethought that goes into choosing a name for the baby. Human-sounding dog names are so popular that it's often hard to tell who's who on the family holiday card: Which one's Emma? The toddler or the terrier? These solid, but sweet, and easy-to-shout names are totally "in" with parents of puppies and babies alike.

FEMALE

- Abby
- Allie
- Annie
- Bonnie
- Carrie
- Cassie
- Chelsea
- Chloe
- Cleo
- Clementine
- Daisy
- Daphne
- Ella
- Ellie
- Emma
- Gemma
- Grace
- Holly
- Lacey
- Lucy
- Lily
- Lola
- Jesse*
- Jordan*
- Maggie
- Maya
- Mia
- Molly
- Phoebe
- Polly
- Poppy
- Riley*
- Sadie
- Samantha
- Shelby
- Sierra
- Skyler
- Sophie
- Zoe

*Could be male or female

MALE

- Alex
- Bailey*
- Brett
- Cassidy*
- Casey*
- Carter
- Charlie
- Chase
- Cody
- Colby*
- Cory
- Dylan*
- Douglas
- Eli
- Gus
- Harley
- Hunter
- Jack
- Jake
- Jackson
- Jesse
- Max
- Oscar
- Rider
- Shane
- Simon
- Spencer
- Teddy
- Theo
- Travis
- Trevor
- Tucker
- Walker
- Zach

Sassy Lassies

Having a female dog gives you the opportunity to pick a name with a little *joie de vie*. These minx-y monikers are more often chosen by showgirls than for schoolgirls—they can be considered a little risqué. But if you've got a pup with a lot of pep and personality, one of these names could be a fine, fun choice.

- Amoré
- Aphrodite
- Babette
- Bambi
- Bijou
- Brandy
- Desirée
- Candy
- Cherie
- Cherry
- Coco
- Coquette
- Diva
- Dixie
- Fifi
- Foxy
- Gigi
- Giselle
- Jezebel
- Lola
- Lulu
- Mamie
- Minx
- Moxie
- Roxie
- Salome
- Scarlett
- Sheba
- Tallulah
- Trixie
- Velvet
- Venus
- Viva
- Vixen
- Zsa Zsa

Geek Chic

Choosing your dog's name is delightfully free of the many difficulties encountered when naming a human child. No matter what name you choose, your dog will never suffer a moment of psychological trauma about it. Your dog won't get teased by other dogs at the park because his name is Melvin. He will never insist on using his initials because his full name is too embarrassing. He will never feel the need to change his name to further his career as a rock star. All of which makes it perfectly fine to give your dog a name few parents have burdened a child with in decades. Despite what your parents may say, it's in no way disrespectful to name your dog after Grandma Mildred. And names that may sound unfashionable on a person can actually be quite chic on a dog.

THE LADIES

- Agatha
- Agnes
- Bertha
- Betty
- Blanche
- Clovis
- Dinah
- Dorcas
- Doris
- Edith
- Edna
- Ethel
- Eunice
- Gertrude
- Gladys
- Henrietta
- Hetty
- Hilda
- Hortense
- Irma
- Madge
- Melba
- Mildred
- Muriel
- Myrtice
- Nellie
- Norma
- Phyllis
- Prudence
- Shirley
- Thelma
- Wilhelmina
- Winifred

THE FELLAS

- Aloysius
- Arnold
- Archie
- Barney
- Delbert
- Cecil
- Clarence
- Clyde
- Edgar
- Ernest
- Floyd
- Godfrey
- Grover
- Irving
- Harold
- Harvey
- Herman
- Homer
- Horace
- Hubert
- Jethro
- Leopold
- Marvin
- Melvin
- Merle
- Milton
- Moe
- Murray
- Orson
- Orville
- Poindexter
- Ralph
- Rufus
- Seymour
- Sherman
- Stanley
- Ugo
- Virgil
- Waldo
- Willard

Let Us Now Praise Famous Humans

Music Makers

What more fitting tribute to your favorite musician than to choose his or her name for your dog? The choices in this category are as wide and varied as the types of music and types of dogs in the world. Some dogs are classical, some operatic—and then there are the very rare, very cool dogs that just ooze improvisational jazz. What kind of beautiful music will your dog make?

- ◯ Amadeus
- ◯ Aretha
- ◯ Bach
- ◯ Beethoven
- ◯ Berlioz
- ◯ Big Boi
- ◯ Billie
- ◯ Bing
- ◯ Björk
- ◯ Bo Diddley
- ◯ Bono
- ◯ Bowie
- ◯ Cab
- ◯ Caruso
- ◯ Chopin
- ◯ Clapton
- ◯ Charo
- ◯ Cher
- ◯ Cobain
- ◯ Coltrane
- ◯ Coolie
- ◯ Dizzy
- ◯ Django
- ◯ Dylan
- ◯ Ellington
- ◯ Elton
- ◯ Elvis
- ◯ Emmylou
- ◯ Fergie
- ◯ Figaro
- ◯ Gershwin
- ◯ Hendrix
- ◯ Howling Wolf
- ◯ Jagger
- ◯ J. Lo
- ◯ Jay-Z

- ○ Jelly Roll
- ○ Jerry
- ○ JoJo
- ○ Joplin
- ○ Keb' Mo'
- ○ Lead Belly
- ○ Lightnin'
- ○ Lil' Bow Wow
- ○ Liszt
- ○ Ludacris
- ○ Ludwig
- ○ Maceo
- ○ Madonna
- ○ Marley
- ○ Mingus
- ○ Muddy Waters
- ○ P. Diddy
- ○ Pachelbel
- ○ Prince
- ○ Puccini
- ○ Reba
- ○ Ringo
- ○ Saffire
- ○ Satchmo
- ○ Shakira
- ○ Shania
- ○ Shubert

- ○ Sinatra
- ○ Snoop Dog
- ○ Sting
- ○ T-Bone
- ○ Thelonious
- ○ Veloso
- ○ Verdi
- ○ Wagner
- ○ Wu-Tang
- ○ Yanni
- ○ Yo Yo Ma
- ○ Zappa
- ○ Zucchero

Musical Terms

- Aida
- Adagio
- Allegra (o)
- Andante
- Aria
- Banjo
- Basso
- Bazooka
- Blues
- Brio
- Bugle

- Calypso
- Cantata
- Caprice
- Didgeridoo
- Fandango
- Hurdy Gurdy
- Kazoo
- Lyric
- Mamba
- Mambo
- Marimba

- Melody
- Oboe
- Piccolo
- Riff
- Sax
- Serenade
- Sonata
- Soprano
- Tango
- Tempo
- Tuba

Note: a endings for female; o endings for male

Famous Dancers

- Alvin
- Balanchine
- Baryshnikov
- Fred
- Ginger
- Isadora

- Merce
- Nijinsky
- Nureyev
- Pavlova
- Twyla

Dog Stars

Looking for a name with star quality? Try one from this list of famous actors and directors.

- Angelina
- Cary Grant
- Gable
- Bardot
- Benigni
- Bergman
- Bertolucci
- Bogie
- Brando
- Cagney
- Capra
- Chaplin
- Clint
- Clooney
- Cocteau
- Cooper
- Coppola
- Charlize
- Demi
- Ewan
- Denzel
- Doris
- Garbo
- Goldie
- Goddard
- Groucho
- Halle
- Hitchcock
- Harlow
- Harpo
- Hepburn
- Hopper
- Jackie Chan
- Keanu
- Keira
- Kurosawa
- Kubrick
- Lucy Liu
- Marilyn
- Orson
- Pacino
- Scorsese
- Sophia Loren
- Spike
- Stallone
- Tarantino
- Travolta
- Truffaut
- Uma
- Valentino
- Viggo
- Woody

Art Dogs

Your dog is cultured, refined, a work of art in herself. An artist's name could really capture those qualities and let your dog leave her mark on the world.

- ○ Alto
- ○ Ansel
- ○ Brâncusi
- ○ Braque
- ○ Bruegel
- ○ Calder
- ○ Caravaggio
- ○ Cezanne
- ○ Constable
- ○ Dali
- ○ Da Vinci
- ○ Degas
- ○ Delacroix
- ○ Donatello
- ○ Duchamp
- ○ Eames
- ○ Eero
- ○ El Greco
- ○ Frida
- ○ Gaugin

- ○ Gehry
- ○ Haring
- ○ Hieronymus
- ○ Hiroshige
- ○ Goya
- ○ Kandinsky
- ○ Klimt
- ○ Magritte
- ○ Matisse
- ○ Michelangelo
- ○ Mies
- ○ Miro
- ○ Modigliani
- ○ Monet

- ○ Noguchi
- ○ Raphael
- ○ Rembrandt
- ○ Remington
- ○ Renoir
- ○ Rodin
- ○ Picasso
- ○ Sargent
- ○ Titian
- ○ Warhol
- ○ Weegee
- ○ Whistler
- ○ Van Gogh
- ○ Velázquez
- ○ Vermeer

Author! Author!

Not only do they produce great literature, they've got great names. Choosing the name of a great auteur for your dog tells the world "My dog is special" and "I know how to read." While you may indeed be a big fan of Joyce Carol Oates, it's best to pick the name of a venerable, old author whom everyone knows by a single name. Dead poets are a popular choice, but if they're not your style, there's nothing wrong with a Clancy, Grisham, or even a King.

- ○ Albee
- ○ Auden
- ○ Austen
- ○ Balzac
- ○ Baudelaire
- ○ Beckett
- ○ Blake
- ○ Boccaccio
- ○ Borges
- ○ Bukowski
- ○ Burroughs
- ○ Brontë
- ○ Byron
- ○ Camus
- ○ Capote
- ○ Casanova
- ○ Cervantes
- ○ Cheever
- ○ Chekhov
- ○ Chaucer
- ○ Clancy
- ○ Cocteau
- ○ Colette
- ○ Dante
- ○ Dashiell
- ○ Defoe
- ○ Dickens
- ○ Dostoyevsky
- ○ Dumas
- ○ Eliot
- ○ Ezra
- ○ Fitzgerald
- ○ Flaubert
- ○ Frost
- ○ Gide
- ○ Goëthe
- ○ Gorky
- ○ Grisham
- ○ Hardy
- ○ Hemingway
- ○ Hugo
- ○ Ibsen
- ○ Huxley
- ○ Joyce
- ○ Kafka
- ○ Keats
- ○ Kerouac
- ○ Kesey
- ○ Kipling
- ○ Langston
- ○ Longfellow
- ○ Lorca
- ○ Mamet
- ○ Neruda

- ○ Márquez
- ○ Pepys
- ○ Pinter
- ○ Poe
- ○ Proust
- ○ Rilke
- ○ Rimbaud
- ○ Rumi
- ○ Salinger
- ○ Saramago
- ○ Sarte
- ○ Seuss
- ○ Shakespeare
- ○ Shelley
- ○ Tennessee
- ○ Tennyson
- ○ Thackeray
- ○ Thoreau
- ○ Tolkien
- ○ Tolstoy
- ○ Twain
- ○ Walt
- ○ Wilde
- ○ Woolf
- ○ Wordsworth
- ○ Yeats
- ○ Zola

Sporting Group

Strength, speed, agility—does your dog possess these traits, along with that intangible element, charisma? If so, a sports star name might be just the ticket. Then again, turnabout is fair play: Calling a dachshund Shaq or a basset hound Ali will certainly score you some points for sense of humor.

○ Aggasi
○ Ali
○ Apolo
○ A-Rod
○ Babe
○ Barkley
○ Beckham
○ Bjorn
○ Bode
○ Camacho
○ Chavez

○ Dr. J
○ El Duce
○ Elway
○ Flutie
○ Gretsky
○ Hank Aaron
○ Honus
○ DiMaggio
○ Gipper
○ Jackie
○ Jordan

- Kareem
- Lance
- LeBron
- Magic
- Madden
- Maradona
- Montana
- Nomar
- Pelé
- Picabo
- Peyton
- Pippen
- Ripkin
- Ronaldinho
- Satchel
- Shaq
- Smokin' Joe
- Sugar Ray
- Tiger
- Venus

Pro Wrestler Names

Fake wrestlers with fake names are a lot of fun.

- ○ 2 Cold Scorpio
- ○ Baby Nitro
- ○ Bam Bam Bigelow
- ○ Blitzkrieg
- ○ Big Guido
- ○ Bulldozer
- ○ Cactus Jack
- ○ Chilly Willy
- ○ Ciclope
- ○ Dino Casanova
- ○ Disco Inferno
- ○ El Dandy
- ○ El Hombre Sin Nombre
- ○ El Terrible
- ○ Hulk Hogan
- ○ Italian Stallion
- ○ Junkyard Dog
- ○ Krusher Kong
- ○ Lady Blossom
- ○ Lash LaRue
- ○ Loch Ness
- ○ Madusa
- ○ Maestro
- ○ Midajah
- ○ Mr. Mexico
- ○ Nature Boy
- ○ Nitro Girl
- ○ Paizley
- ○ Rhino
- ○ Road Warrior
- ○ Starla Saxton
- ○ Super Calo
- ○ Tarzan Boy
- ○ The Tazmaniac
- ○ Tigre Blanco
- ○ Ze Gangsta

Brainiacs

If your dog figured out how to put on his own leash and take himself for a walk on his first day home, you may be dealing with a dog genius. It might be wise to consider a name from one of the giants of science, math, and physics.

- ○ Archimedes
- ○ Asimov
- ○ Banneker
- ○ Cassini
- ○ Copernicus
- ○ Cousteau
- ○ Curie
- ○ Darwin
- ○ Doppler
- ○ Edison
- ○ Einstein
- ○ Euclid
- ○ Faraday
- ○ Foucault
- ○ Hubble
- ○ Galileo
- ○ Gutenberg
- ○ Kepler
- ○ Marconi
- ○ Mendel
- ○ Newton
- ○ Ohm
- ○ Pascal
- ○ Pavlov
- ○ Pliny
- ○ Tesla
- ○ Tycho

Is There a Dog?

Certain dogs just have that look on their face—the one that says "Quiet, please, I'm contemplating the meaning of the universe." If your dog is a deep thinker, consider one of these weighty names.

- ○ Aristotle
- ○ Cassius
- ○ Chomsky
- ○ Cicero
- ○ Confucius
- ○ Descartes
- ○ Emerson
- ○ Freud
- ○ Heidegger
- ○ Homer

- ○ Hume
- ○ Jung
- ○ Kierkegaard
- ○ Kant
- ○ Machiavelli
- ○ Nietzsche
- ○ Ovid
- ○ Philo
- ○ Plato
- ○ Plutarch

- ○ Rousseau
- ○ Sartre
- ○ Seneca
- ○ Siddhartha
- ○ Socrates
- ○ Spinoza
- ○ Thoreau
- ○ Virgil
- ○ Voltaire

Top Dogs

Political Pooches

It's lonely at the top. Heavy is the head that wears the crown. Loyalty is in short supply in the world of politics, so it's no wonder many leaders keep the most faithful of creatures at their side. History is full of dogs that have trotted through the halls of power—why not choose one of these famous names for your very own special advisor?

Pets of U.S. Presidents and Their Families

NAME	BREED	OWNER
Barney	Scottish Terrier	George W. Bush
Beagle	Beagle	Lyndon Johnson
Bessie	Collie	Calvin Coolidge
Big Ben	Fox Terrier	Herbert Hoover
Blackberry	Chow	Calvin Coolidge
Blanco	Collie	Lyndon Johnson
Blaze	Bull Mastiff	Elliot Roosevelt
Boston Beans	Bulldog	Calvin Coolidge
Bruce	Bull Terrier	Woodrow Wilson
Buddy	Chocolate Lab	Bill Clinton
Calamity Jane	Shetland Sheepdog	Calvin Coolidge

NAME	BREED	OWNER
○ Charlie	Welsh Terrier	Caroline Kennedy
○ Checkers	Cocker Spaniel	Richard Nixon
○ Clipper	German Shepherd	John F. Kennedy
○ Dash	Unknown	Benjamin Harrison
○ Davie	Airedale	Woodrow Wilson
○ Deke	English Mastiff	Rutherford B. Hayes
○ Dot	Cocker Spaniel	Rutherford B. Hayes
○ Drunkard	Black and Tan Hound	George Washington
○ Eaglehurst	Gillette Setter	Herbert Hoover
○ Fala	Scottish Terrier	Franklin D. Roosevelt
○ Feller	Cocker Spaniel	Harry Truman
○ Fido	Mutt	Abraham Lincoln
○ Glen	Scotch Collie	Herbert Hoover
○ Grim	Greyhound	Rutherford B. Hayes
○ Hector	Newfoundland	Rutherford B. Hayes
○ Him	Beagle	Lyndon Johnson
○ Heidi	Weimaraner	Dwight Eisenhower
○ Her	Beagle	Lyndon Johnson
○ Jack	Manchester Terrier	Theodore Roosevelt

NAME	BREED	OWNER
◯ Juno	Unknown	John Adams and Rutherford B. Hayes
◯ King Tut	German Shepherd	Herbert Hoover
◯ King Timahoe	Irish Setter	Richard Nixon
◯ Laddie Buck	Airedale	Calvin Coolidge
◯ Le Beau	Italian Greyhound	John Tyler
◯ Liberty	Golden Retriever	Gerald Ford
◯ Little Beagle	Beagle	Lyndon Johnson
◯ Lucky	Bouvier des Flandres	Ronald Reagan
◯ Major	German Shepherd	Franklin D. Roosevelt
◯ Madam Moose	Dalmation	George Washington
◯ Meggie	Scottish Terrier	Franklin D. Roosevelt
◯ Millie	Springer Spaniel	Barbara Bush
◯ Miss Beazley	Scottish Terrier	George W. Bush
◯ Manchu	Pekinese	Alice Roosevelt
◯ Mountain Boy	Greyhound	Woodrow Wilson
◯ Palo Alto	Unknown	Calvin Coolidge
◯ Pasha	Terrier	Richard Nixon
◯ Paul Pry	Airedale	Calvin Coolidge
◯ Patrick	Irish Wolfhound	Herbert Hoover
◯ Pete	Bull Terrier	Theodore Roosevelt
◯ President	Great Dane	Franklin D. Roosevelt

NAME	BREED	OWNER
○ Prudence Prim	Collie	Calvin Coolidge
○ Pushnika	Mutt	Caroline Kennedy
○ Rex	Cavalier King Charles Spaniel	Ronald Reagan
○ Rob Roy	Collie	Calvin Coolidge
○ Rosie	Unknown	Ulysses S. Grant
○ Rollo	St. Bernard	Theodore Roosevelt
○ Ruby Rough	Collie	Calvin Coolidge
○ Sailor Boy	Chesapeake Bay Retriever	Theodore Roosevelt
○ Scentwell	Unknown	George Washington
○ Seamus	Unknown	Bill Clinton
○ Shannon	Irish Spaniel	Caroline Kennedy
○ Skip	Rat Terrier	Theodore Roosevelt
○ Sonnie	Fox Terrier	Herbert Hoover
○ Spotty Fetcher	English Springer Spaniel	George W. Bush
○ Taster	Black and Tan Coonhound	George Washington
○ Tiny	Old English Sheepdog	Franklin D. Roosevelt
○ Tipler	Black and Tan Coonhound	George Washington
○ Tipsy	Black and Tan Hound	George Washington

NAME	BREED	OWNER
◯ Sweet Lips	Staghound	George Washington
◯ Veto	Unknown	James Garfield
◯ Vicky	Poodle	Richard Nixon
◯ Vulcan	Staghound	George Washington
◯ Weeje	Norwegian Wolfhound	Herbert Hoover
◯ Winks	Llewellyn Setter	Franklin D. Roosevelt
◯ Wolf	Mutt	John F. Kennedy
◯ Yuki	Mutt	Lyndon Johnson
◯ Yukon	Malamute	Herbert Hoover

The Queen's Corgis and Dorgis

Names of Her Majesty Queen Elizabeth of England's dogs (includes current and former pets).

◯ Berry
◯ Brandy
◯ Cider
◯ Emma
◯ Fable
◯ Flora
◯ Harris

◯ Holly
◯ Kelpie
◯ Linnet
◯ Minnie
◯ Monty
◯ Myth

◯ Roseval Golden Eagle
◯ Rush
◯ Pharos
◯ Swift
◯ Willow

Best of the Rest

NAME	BREED	OWNER
○ Baltique	Unknown	François Mitterrand
○ Boy	Dachshund	Queen Victoria
○ Caesar	Wire Fox Terrier	King Edward VII
○ Dash	Dachshund	Queen Victoria
○ Diamond	Pomeranian	Sir Isaac Newton
○ Fortune	Pug	Empress Josephine Bonaparte
○ Genouille	Dachshund	Napoleon
○ Hamlet	Unknown	Sir Walter Scott
○ Inez	Unknown	Madame de Pompadour
○ Jack	Terrier	Duke of Wellington
○ Maida	Scottish Deerhound	Sir Walter Scott
○ Mathe	Greyhound	Richard II
○ Mimi	Papillon	Madame de Pompadour
○ Nimrod	Bloodhound	Sir Walter Scott
○ Peritas	Unknown	Alexander the Great
○ Pompe	Unknown	Charles XII of Sweden

NAME	BREED	OWNER
○ Rogue	Unknown	Charles I of France
○ Rufus	Poodle	Winston Churchill
○ Seaman	Newfoundland	Meriwether Lewis
○ Torm	Scottish Deerhound	Lord Colonsay of Scotland
○ Urian	Wolfhound	Anne Boleyn
○ Vic	Terrier	Duke of Wellington

Best in Show Winners

Best in Show. It's the ultimate prize for pedigree dogs and their handlers. The top dogs at the top shows win not only the admiration of the crowds, but a spot in history. A dog's name might not have much to do with whether or not he takes a place on the podium, but as it happens, some of the most distinctive dogs also have distinctive names. Most dogs carry the name of their trainers or kennel as part of their "official" name, which explains the length of many of these winning monikers. Consider choosing all or part of these blue-ribbon names. Or use them as inspiration to create a prize-winning name for your own little champ.

Westminster Dog Show Winners

NAME	BREED
○ Warren Remedy	Fox Terrier
○ Sabine Rarebit	Fox Terrier
○ Tickle 'Em Jock	Scottish Terrier
○ Kenmore Sorceress	Airedale
○ Strathway Prince Albert	Bulldog
○ Brentwood Hero	Old English Sheepdog
○ Matford Vic	Old English Sheepdog
○ Comejo Wycollar Boy	Fox Terrier
○ Haymarket Faultless	Bull Terrier
○ Briergate Bright Beauty	Airedale
○ Midkiff Seductive	Cocker Spaniel
○ Boxwood Barkentine	Airedale
○ Barberryhill Bootlegger	Sealyham

NAME	BREED
○ Governor Moscow	Pointer
○ Signal Circuit	Fox Terrier
○ Pinegrade Perfection	Sealyham
○ Talavera Margaret	Fox Terrier
○ Land Loyalty of Bellhaven	Collie
○ Pendley Calling of Blarney	Fox Terrier
○ Nancolleth Markable	Pointer
○ Warland Protector of Shelterock	Airedale
○ Flornell Spicy Bit of Halleston	Fox Terrier
○ Nunsoe Duc de la Terrace of Blakeen	Standard Poodle
○ St. Margaret Magnificent of Clairedale	Sealyham
○ Flornell Spicy Bit of Halleston	Fox Terrier
○ Daro of Maridor	English Setter
○ Ferry Von Rauhfelsen of Giralda	Doberman
○ My Own Brucie	Cocker Spaniel
○ Wolvey Pattern of Edgerstoune	West Highland Terrier
○ Pitter Patter of Piperscroft	Miniature Poodle
○ Flornell Rarebit of Twin Ponds	Welsh Terrier
○ Shieling's Signature	Scottish Terrier

NAME	BREED
○ Hetherington Model Rhythm	Fox Terrier
○ Warlord of Mazelaine	Boxer
○ Rock Ridge Night Rocket	Bedlington Terrier
○ Mazelaine's Zazarac Brandy	Boxer
○ Walsing Winning Trick of Edgerstoune	Scottish Terrier
○ Bang Away of Sirrah Crest	Boxer
○ Rancho Dobe's Storm	Doberman
○ Carmor's Rise and Shine	Cocker Spaniel
○ Kippax Fearnought	Bulldog
○ Wilber White Swan	Toy Poodle
○ Shirkhan of Grandeur	Afghan Hound
○ Puttencove Promise	Standard Poodle
○ Fontclair Festoon	Miniature Poodle
○ Chick T'Sun of Caversham	Pekingese
○ Cappoquin Little Sister	Toy Poodle
○ Elfinbrook Simon	West Highland Terrier
○ Wakefield's Black Knight	English Springer Spaniel
○ Courtenay Fleetfoot of Pennyworth	Whippet
○ Carmichael's Fanfare	Scottish Terrier
○ Zeloy Mooremaides Magic	Fox Terrier

NAME	BREED
◯ Bardene Bingo	Scottish Terrier
◯ Stingray of Derryabah	Lakeland Terrier
◯ Glamoor Good News	Skye Terrier
◯ Arriba's Prima Donna	Boxer
◯ Chinoe's Adamant James	English Springer Spaniel
◯ Acadia Command Performance	Standard Poodle
◯ Gretchenh of Columbia River	German Shorthaired Pointer
◯ Sir Lancelot of Barvan	Old English Sheepdog
◯ Jo Ni's Red Baron of Crofton	Lakeland Terrier
◯ Dersade Bobby's Girl	Sealyham Terrier
◯ Cede Higgens	Yorkshire Terrier
◯ Oak Tree's Irishtocrat	Irish Water Spaniel
◯ Sierra Cinnar	Siberian Husky
◯ Dhandy Favorite Woodchuck	Pug
◯ St. Aubrey Dragonora of Elsdon	Pekingese
◯ Kabik's the Challenger	Afghan Hound
◯ Seaward's Blackbeard	Newfoundland
◯ Braeburn's Close Encounter	Scottish Terrier
◯ Marjetta National Acclaim	Pointer
◯ Covy Tucker Hill's Manhattan	German Shepherd

NAME	BREED
⦾ Great Elms Prince Charming II	Pomeranian
⦾ Royal Tudor's Wild as the Wind	Doberman
⦾ Wendessa Crown Prince	Pekingese
⦾ Whisperwind on a Carousel	Standard Poodle
⦾ Lonesome Dove	Fox Terrier
⦾ Salilyn's Condor	English Springer Spaniel
⦾ Chidley Willum	Norwich Terrier
⦾ Gaelforce Post Script	Scottish Terrier
⦾ Clussex Country Sunrise	Clumber Spaniel
⦾ Parsifal di Casa Netzer	Standard Schnauzer
⦾ Fairewood Frolic	Norwich Terrier
⦾ Loteki's Supernatural Being	Papillion
⦾ Salilyn 'N Erin's Shameless	English Springer Spaniel
⦾ Special Times Just Right	Bichon Frisé
⦾ Surrey Spice Girl	Miniature Poodle
⦾ Torum's Scarf Michael	Kerry Blue Terrier
⦾ Darbydale's All Rise Pouchcove	Newfoundland
⦾ Kan-Point's VJK Autumn Roses	German Shorthaired Pointer
⦾ Rocky Top's Sundance Kid	Bull Terrier

Celebrity Hounds

Celebrities have the best of everything—the best salaries, the best houses, and some think, the best dog names. Since nothing's too good for your dog, why not consider one of these A-list names for your own little doggie diva?

NAME	CELEB
○ Atticus and Boo Radley	Jake Gyllenhaal
○ Baci and Petals	Sigourney Weaver
○ Barbie	Venus Williams
○ Bea, Buster, Jet, Red, Tussem, and Zen	Kelsey Grammar
○ Bearlie and Bella	Justin Timberlake
○ Bing and Bong	Mariah Carey
○ Bizkit	Fred Durst
○ Bubba	Minnie Driver
○ Buttermilk and Shug	Ashley Judd
○ Centaur Pendragon and Kabar	Rudolph Valentino
○ Ceelo	Adrien Brody
○ Cheeseburger	Jimmy Buffett
○ Chester	Fran Drescher
○ Ching-Ching II	Shirley Temple
○ Chiquita	Madonna
○ Clara Bo	Kate Hudson
○ Cyrus	Drea de Matteo
○ Daisy	Jessica Simpson
○ Debutante	Peri Gilpin
○ Denver and Delilah	Charlize Theron
○ Dodo	Ivana Trump

NAME	CELEB
○ Enzo	Jennifer Aniston
○ Dudley	Mary Tyler Moore
○ Finoula	Billy Joel
○ Flossie, Vivian, and Templeton	Drew Barrymore
○ Holden	Gwyneth Paltrow
○ Hooper and Hardy	Courtney Cox and David Arquette
○ J.J.	Noah Wyle
○ Jinxy	Eva Longoria
○ Junior	Lucille Ball
○ Luca	Mary Kate Olsen
○ Mafia	Marilyn Monroe
○ Maggie	Scarlett Johansson
○ Milo	Diane Lane
○ Miss Hudd	Matthew McConaughey
○ Moise and Mo	Rupert Everett
○ Mr. Famous	Audrey Hepburn
○ Norman	Jennifer Aniston
○ Oliver	Nicolette Sheridan
○ Pelé	Melissa Joan Hart
○ Poppy	Tim Burton
○ Porgy and Bess	Sienna Miller
○ Precious	David Hasselhoff
○ Raindrops	Rosie Perez
○ Raven	LeeAnn Rimes
○ Rufus	Leonardo DiCaprio

NAME	CELEB
⚪ Puggy Sue	Paula Abdul
⚪ Samson	Alicia Silverstone
⚪ Sid and Nancy	Jessica Alba
⚪ Sidi	Orlando Bloom
⚪ Sophie and Solomon	Oprah Winfrey
⚪ Tinkerbell	Paris Hilton
⚪ Veronica	Joan Rivers
⚪ Walden	Matt Lauer
⚪ Winston	Gavin Rosdale
⚪ Woof	Renée Zellweger
⚪ Zhaki, Ludo, and Indo	Will Smith
⚪ Zukelia Dobson, Blue Maximillian, Genghis Khan Chin-Chin, Kublai Khan Paw-Paw	Martha Stewart

Power Dogs

Some dogs don't need a famous human as a sidekick—
they're famous in their own right. Famous athletes, heroes,
and loyal friends, these dogs are inspiring. Who knows what
great deeds your dog might achieve with a name like one
of these?

NAME	CLAIM TO FAME
○ Adjutant	Reportedly the oldest dog ever; lived to age 28
○ Aibe	Famous wolfhound in Irish legend
○ Ashley Whippet	First "disc dog superstar"
○ Balto and Togo	Sled dogs who delivered diphtheria antitoxin to Nome, Alaska, during a blizzard, preventing an epidemic
○ Barry	Famous St. Bernard who rescued 41 people in an avalanche
○ Chinook	Team leader for the Byrd Antarctic Expeditions

NAME	CLAIM TO FAME
○ Bouhaki	Ancient dog of Thebes found entombed with his master
○ Brutus	Famous skydiving mini dachshund
○ Bud Nelson	First dog to travel across the U.S. in an automobile
○ Battina, Chip, Chundo Crooky, Fay Wray, and Man Ray	Weimaraners made famous by William Wegman's photographs of them
○ Canton	Matriarch of the Chesapeake Bay Retriever breed
○ Dorsey	Famous "maildog" of the 19th century

NAME	CLAIM TO FAME
○ Faith	Only known bipedal dog
○ Gelert	Famous dog who died protecting the son of Llewellyn the Great
○ Granite	Lead dog in a record-breaking Iditarod race
○ Greyfriar's Bobby	Famously loyal dog who waited by his master's grave for years, subject of a book and movie
○ Hachiko	Famously loyal dog who waited for his master at a train station in Japan for 11 years
○ Handsome Dan	Yale University mascot
○ Igloo	Wire Fox Terrier who accompanied Admiral Byrd on his polar expeditions
○ Kurwenal	Trained dog said to have the intelligence of a human 10 year old
○ Mancs	Famous rescue dog who saved many lives
○ Old Shep	Famously loyal dog who waited at a train station for his master for five years
○ Owney	Official U.S. Postal Service dog of the 19th century
○ Rico	Famous "talking" dog

NAME	CLAIM TO FAME
◯ Robot	Dog who discovered the cave paintings in Lascaux, France
◯ Spareribs	Famous U.S Army parachuting dog
◯ Snuppy	First cloned dog
◯ Uga	University of Georgia mascot
◯ Zorba	English Mastiff holding the title of World's Heaviest Dog

Dogs of War

None of those cutesy dog names for you—your dog's a tough guy, the kind of dog who eats poodles for lunch (metaphorically speaking, of course). If you're looking for a dog name that says "proceed with caution," one of these alpha-dog, military-inspired names might just be for you. They're especially popular with owners of rottweilers, bulldogs, dobermans, and the like. On the other hand, a name like Spike could be pretty funny on a chihuahua or a chow.

- ○ Ace
- ○ Admiral
- ○ Alpha
- ○ Ammo
- ○ Attila
- ○ Baron
- ○ Bazooka
- ○ Beretta
- ○ Blade
- ○ Blitz
- ○ Braveheart
- ○ Bravo
- ○ Bullet
- ○ Caesar
- ○ Captain
- ○ Chief
- ○ Chopper
- ○ Colonel
- ○ Colt
- ○ Commodore
- ○ Corps
- ○ Deuce
- ○ Duke
- ○ Fang
- ○ Flyboy
- ○ G.I.
- ○ Grunt
- ○ Hero
- ○ Honch
- ○ Howitzer
- ○ Hulk
- ○ Humvee
- ○ Hummer
- ○ Hunter
- ○ Ike
- ○ Jag
- ○ Kamikaze
- ○ Killer
- ○ Liberty
- ○ Major

- ◯ Magnum
- ◯ MacArthur
- ◯ Matador
- ◯ Ninja
- ◯ Maverick
- ◯ Outlaw
- ◯ Panzer
- ◯ Patriot
- ◯ Patton
- ◯ Pershing
- ◯ Pistol
- ◯ Raider
- ◯ Ranger
- ◯ Rambo
- ◯ Red Baron
- ◯ Remington
- ◯ Rocky
- ◯ Rocco
- ◯ Rocket
- ◯ Ranger
- ◯ Samurai
- ◯ Sarge
- ◯ Semper Fi
- ◯ Sherman
- ◯ Slugger
- ◯ Spartan
- ◯ Spike
- ◯ Squid
- ◯ Striker
- ◯ Stinger
- ◯ Stetson
- ◯ Tank
- ◯ Titan
- ◯ Trooper
- ◯ Vulcan
- ◯ Warrior

Famous War Dogs

NAME	CLAIM TO FAME
◯ Bamse	St. Bernard who served the Free Norwegian Forces during World War II
◯ Chips	World War II dog hero
◯ Horrie the Wog-Dog	Australian dog hero of World War II
◯ Judy	Dog hero of the British Navy in World War II
◯ Just Nuisance	Only dog officially enlisted in the Royal Navy
◯ Sergeant Stubby	The most decorated U.S. dog hero; served in World War I

Space Dogs

The noble canine—what better species to serve as Earth's ambassadors should there really be intelligent life in the Universe? In the early days of the Soviet space program, dogs boldly went where no man had been before—into orbit outside the Earth's atmosphere. These space dogs, as they came to be known, earned a place in history with their heroic journeys into the great unknown. If your dog has an adventurous spirit, one of these space dog names might be just the ticket.

DOG	MEANING	MISSION
○ Albina	Whitey	Sub-orbital flight
○ Bars	Panther or Lynx	Test flight
○ Belka	Squirrel	Sputnik 5
○ Chernushka	Blackie	Sputnik 9
○ Damka	Little Lady	Sub-orbital flight
○ Krasavka	Beauty	Sub-orbital flight
○ Laika	Husky or Barker	Sputnik 2
(First animal to orbit the Earth)		
○ Lisa	Vixen	Sub-orbital flight
○ Lisichka	Little Fox	Test flight
○ Malyshka	Little One	Sub-orbital flight
○ Modnista	Fashionable	Sub-orbital flight
○ Mushka	Little Fly	Sputnik 6
○ Muttnik	American nick-name for Laika	Sputnik 2

DOG	MEANING	MISSION
◯ Otvazhnaya	Brave One	Sub-orbital flight
◯ Pchelka	Little Bee	Sputnik 6
◯ Ryjik	Ginger	Sub-orbital flight
◯ Smelaya	Brave	Sub-orbital flight

(Trained as astronaut, but ran off the day before her first flight)

◯ Strelka	Little Arrow	Sputnik 5
◯ Tsyganka	Gypsy girl	Sub-orbital flight
◯ Ugolyok	Little Piece of Coal	Vokshod 3

(Shares "longest canine space flight" record with Veterok)

◯ Veterok	Little Wind	Vokshod 3
◯ Zvezdochka	Little Star	Sputnik 10

Long Live Laika

Perhaps the most famous space dog was Laika, whose name means "Husky" or "Barker" in Russian. Laika had lots of nicknames, including Kudryavka (Little Curly), Zhuchka (Little Beetle), Limonchik (Little Lemon), and Muttnik. She was a stray, picked up from the streets of Moscow and catapulted, not only into the international spotlight, but also into outer space, when she became the first earthling to orbit the Earth. Laika was put aboard the Sputnik 2, which blasted out of the Earth's atmosphere on November 3, 1957. Laika didn't make it back to Earth alive; in fact, there wasn't even a re-entry strategy for her mission. Although some Soviet reports claimed she lived for days in space, in 2002 it was revealed that she died five to seven hours into her mission from overheating and stress. She was hailed as an international hero for her contribution to space exploration. The scientist responsible for the mission later regretted that more was not done to try to save her.

The Canine Gourmet

Doggie Dishes

There's a veritable smorgasbord of food-related names to choose from for your dog. For folks with simple tastes, there are names like Cookie and Hoagie. Those with a more sophisticated palate might consider a Truffle or Pâté. Exotic names such as Tikka or Dobosch (a Hungarian cake) might just whet your appetite if you're a dog lover and a culinary adventurer.

- Bonbon
- Brie
- Calamari
- Caramel
- Cayenne
- Chai
- Chili
- Chapati
- Chips
- Cider
- Cocoa
- Coffee
- Cola
- Cookie
- Dijon
- Dobosch
- Emmenthal
- Étouffée
- Feta
- Fondu
- Garbanzo
- Ginger
- Ginseng
- Gouda
- Gumbo
- Grits
- Gyro
- Hoagie
- Java
- Kiwi
- Kona
- Kumquat
- Jalapeño
- Java
- Latte
- Limburger
- Manchego
- Marmalade
- Marzipan
- Masala
- Maytag
  (blue cheese)
- Marshmallow
- Matzo
- Mignon
- Mocha
- Mutsu (apple)
- Muffin
- Muffelata
- Nilla
- Nougat
- Nutmeg
- Olive
- Oreo
- Paella
- Paprika
- Pâte
- Queso
- Quiche
- Porcini
- Ragù
- Reuben
- Roquefort
- Saffron
- Saga
  (blue cheese)
- Salsa
- Samosa
- Sashimi
- Sassafras
- Sorbet
- Splenda
- Sushi
- Tartine
- Tikka
- Truffle
- Tofu
- Vindaloo
- Wasabi
- Winesap
  (apple)

Spirits

If you thirst for a name with a little "spirit," check out the wine and cocktail list: Sake and Sangria aren't just fun to drink—they're deliciously different names for your dog.

- Amaretto
- Bacardi
- Beaujolais
- Boudreaux
- Calvados
- Captain Morgan
- Cassis
- Chianti
- Cognac
- Cointreau
- Courvoisier
- Cuervo
- Daiquiri
- Drambuie
- Gimlet
- Grog
- Julep
- Kahlúa
- Kamikaze
- Kir

- Pernod
- Pinot
- Madras
- Merlot
- Mai tai
- Martini
- Merlot
- Midori
- Mimosa
- Mojito
- Moonshine
- Ouzo

- Pastis
- Sambuca
- Sake
- Sangria
- Scotch
- Sherry
- Shiraz
- Smirnoff
- Spumante
- Soju
- Tequila
- Toddy
- Whiskey

Bow Wow Bling Bling

Uptown Hound

Urban legends featuring babies called Benz or Lexus abound. Parents are said to choose these chi-chi names as part of an endorsement deal to pay for Junior's college education. Even if hospital nurseries aren't really bursting with babies named for luxury goods, those names are definitely becoming more common at the kennel. With all those vet bills and the price of gourmet dog food (only the best for your pooch!), you may not be able to reach for that top-shelf liquor at the club anymore. And that new puppy might make lunch out of your Manolos. But a bling-bling dog name is a fun way to bring a little luxe into your life without running up your credit card.

- ○ Adidas
- ○ Armani
- ○ Bally
- ○ Beemer
- ○ Beluga
- ○ Benz
- ○ Bentley
- ○ Birken
- ○ Bulgari
- ○ Boss
- ○ Burberry
- ○ Caddy
- ○ Cartier
- ○ Cash
- ○ Cashmere
- ○ Chanel
- ○ Chivas
- ○ Cristal

- Diamond
- Dior
- Dolce
- Ducati
- Fendi
- Godiva
- Gucci
- Hermès
- Hummer
- Jag
- Juicy
- Krug
- Lauren
- Lexus
- Manolo
- Mercedes
- Miu Miu
- Money
- Neiman
- Nike
- Rémy
- Perrier
- Porsche
- Prada
- Puma
- Ritz
- Rolex
- Saks
- Seven
- Stoli
- Tommy
- Versace

Down-Market Doggie

You are not concerned with status symbols. Forget the caviar and Dom Perignon. A can of PBR and a bag of pork rinds are all right by you any time, thank you very much. Right now, blue collar and redneck are red hot, so why not choose a decidedly down-market name for your dog?

- ○ Ace
- ○ Billy Bob
- ○ Bocephus
- ○ Bubba
- ○ Bud
- ○ Butter Bean
- ○ Chevy
- ○ Cletus
- ○ Cleavon
- ○ Cooter
- ○ Dixie
- ○ Dr. Pepper
- ○ Earl
- ○ Freebird
- ○ Harley
- ○ Heinie
- ○ Hog
- ○ Hooch

- ○ Hoppin' John
- ○ Hot Rod
- ○ Huck
- ○ Hush Puppy
- ○ John Boy
- ○ Johnny Cake
- ○ Kegger
- ○ Lester
- ○ Lurlene
- ○ Marlboro
- ○ Moonpie
- ○ Nascar
- ○ Nehi
- ○ PBR
- ○ R.C.
- ○ Piggly Wiggly
- ○ Pimento

- ○ Possum
- ○ Ripple
- ○ Roadie
- ○ Roscoe
- ○ Scooter
- ○ Schlitz
- ○ Shooter
- ○ Shoo Fly
- ○ Six-pack
- ○ Skeeder
- ○ Skynard
- ○ Spam
- ○ Talladega
- ○ Truckstop
- ○ Twinkie
- ○ Whiskey
- ○ Z.Z.

Dungeons, Dragons, and Dogs

When it comes to picking dog names, fantasy fans have a vast and rich field from which to choose. The sheer inventiveness of these names makes them hard to resist. It's far too complicated to explain here the many layers and levels of the fantasy worlds these names come from. If you find one that sounds good, look it up before choosing it for your dog. It might just be the name of a bloodthirsty, half-orc barbarian—perhaps not the right name for your Pomeranian. Then again, that might be just the ironic twist you're looking for.

- ○ Alhana Starbreeze
- ○ Alhamazad the Wise
- ○ Aramil
- ○ Arilyn Moonblade
- ○ Azalin Rex
- ○ Belpheron
- ○ Belwar Dissengulp
- ○ Bigby
- ○ Boddyknock Glinckle
- ○ Bucknard
- ○ Calibast
- ○ Captain Deudermont
- ○ Cireka
- ○ Crysania

- ○ Cyric
- ○ Devis
- ○ Dhamon Grimwulf
- ○ Dorna Trapspringer
- ○ Drogan Droganson
- ○ Dragonbait
- ○ Dragotha
- ○ Drizzt
- ○ Edralve
- ○ Elistan
- ○ Elminster Aumar
- ○ Envid Divine
- ○ Errtu
- ○ Evard
- ○ Fenthick Moss
- ○ Flint Fireforge
- ○ Gareth Dragonsbane
- ○ Gilthas Pathfinder
- ○ Gimble
- ○ Goldmoon
- ○ Gord the Rogue
- ○ Grimgnaw
- ○ Harkle Harpell
- ○ Iggwilv
- ○ Imoen
- ○ Ivan Bouldershoulder
- ○ Jaboli
- ○ Jarlaxle
- ○ Jasla
- ○ Jozan
- ○ Kaidala
- ○ Kargoth
- ○ Karsus
- ○ Kazak
- ○ Kelemvor Lyonsbane
- ○ Keraptis
- ○ Kerwyn
- ○ Kierkan Rufo
- ○ Krusk

- Lady Aribeth
- Leomund
- Lidda
- Maugrim
- Melf
- Morage
- Mordenkainen
- Montolio Debrouchee
- Morthos
- Nerof Gasgal
- Nystul
- Obmi
- Olive Ruskettle
- Otiluke
- Rary
- Regis Rumblebelly
- Robilar
- Riverwind
- Sharwyn
- Snurre Ironbelly
- Sorra

- Steel Brightblade
- Taegan Nightwind
- Tanin
- Tika
- Tasha
- Tasslehoff
- Thibbledorf Pwent
- Tordek
- Usha
- Valen Shadowbreath
- Vandgerdahst
- Vecna
- Warduke
- Warnes Starcoat
- Wulfgar
- Xanos Messarmos
- Xerses
- Ygorl
- Zhai
- Zhengyi

Forces of Nature

As strong as a storm, as gentle as a breeze, as cheerful as a summer day—does one of these describe your pooch? Look to nature for inspiration for names that fit your dog's looks or personality.

- April
- Aurora
- August
- Autumn
- Bay
- Birch
- Blizzard
- Breeze
- Comet
- Coral
- Dawn
- Diamond
- Ebony
- Eclipse
- Echo
- Emerald
- Étoile (French for star)
- Feather
- Fern
- Fire
- Flame
- Forest
- Garnet
- Harbor
- Ice
- Indigo
- Lapis
- Lightning
- Luna
- Jade
- January
- Jasper
- Mariposa (Spanish for butterfly)
- Meadow
- Mica
- Midnight
- Moonlight
- Moonglow
- Misty
- Ocean
- Onyx
- Opal
- Printemps (French for Spring)
- Rain
- Rainbow
- Ruby
- Raven
- River
- September
- Shadow
- Shade
- Sky

- Snowflake
- Soleil (French for sun)
- Summer
- Sunny
- Sunshine
- Stormy
- Star
- Estrella (Spanish for star)
- Thunder
- Twilight
- Twister
- Topaz
- Willow
- Windy

FLORA

- Azalia
- Banyan
- Baobab
- Blossom
- Blackberry
- Blueberry
- Briony
- Clover
- Daisy
- Fern
- Fuchsia
- Hyacinth
- Holly
- Ivy
- Lavender
- Jasmine
- Jonquil
- Magnolia
- Mimosa
- Myrtle
- Lilac
- Pansy
- Petal
- Petunia
- Poppy
- Raspberry
- Rosebud
- Sage
- Sassafras
- Seed
- Sequoia
- Violet

FAUNA

- Badger
- Bear
- Beaver
- Birdy
- Cheetah
- Cougar
- Cobra
- Coyote
- Dove
- Eagle
- Grebe
- Ibis
- Kestrel
- Kiwi
- Koala
- Gator
- Grizzly
- Lark
- Magpie
- Moose
- Monkey
- Oryx
- Panda
- Panther
- Puma
- Raven
- Rooster
- Tiger
- Wolf

Sensitive New Age Dog

Forget the whole Dog of War thing (see page 92)—your dog's all about peace and harmony. You have positive energy, so your dog's name should reflect that. These Eastern-influenced names strike just the right note when you're looking for something a little spiritual and a little different. For a completely unique name, try adding one or more of the names from Forces of Nature (see page 107) to one of the names here: Jade Storm, Violet Crystal, or Moonglow Aura are some magical, mystical combinations.

○ Asia
○ Aries
○ Aquarius
○ Aura
○ Bindi
○ Capricorn
○ Celeste
○ Chai
○ Chakra
○ Chi
○ Crystal
○ Dervish
○ Deva
○ Dharma

○ East
○ Gaia
○ Gemini
○ Gnosis
○ Guru
○ Idduna
○ Isis
○ Kali
○ Kaya
○ Karma
○ Karuna
○ Kali
○ Kokopelli
○ Kundalina

○ Krishna
○ Libra
○ Luna
○ Mandala
○ Mantra
○ Moonbeam
○ Moonfire
○ Mystic
○ Nirvana
○ Om
○ Omega
○ Pachouli
○ Pisces
○ Prajñ

○ Scorpio ○ Spirit ○ Taurus
○ Shalom ○ Sufi ○ Yin
○ Shaman ○ Starbright ○ Yang
○ Shanti ○ Stardust ○ Virgo
○ Swami ○ Stargazer ○ Yogi
○ Swamji ○ Tantra ○ West
○ Shiva ○ Tao ○ Zen
○ Solstice ○ Tarot

Terms of Endearment

It's bound to happen sometime—you'll get caught talking baby talk to your dog. You might not even realize you're doing it until you see the look of horror on your friend's face: *Did you just call your dog Mr. Snuggly-Bottom?* Don't worry—you're in good company. Few dog owners can resist giving their dog an endearing nickname. Chances are, even if you *officially* give your dog another name, you'll end up using a term of endearment (or two or three!) at least part of the time. You can always save these names for those special moments when it's just the two of you.

- Amoré (Italian for love)
- Amor
- Baby
- Bebé
- Babs
- Babykins
- Bambino
- Bobo
- Boo
- Boo Boo
- Buffy
- Bugsy
- Butterball
- Chiquita(o) (Spanish for little one)
- Chubsy-ubsy
- Ciccia (Italian for sweetie)
- Cochita/cochis
- Conlechita/o (Spanish for coffee with milk)
- Corazon (Spanish for heart)
- Crumpet
- Cubby

Note: a endings for female; o endings for male

- Cupcake
- Cuddles
- Curly
- Cutie Pie
- Dolly
- Doodle
- Dumpling
- Honey
- Kewpie
- Kibbles
- Liebshen (German for baby)
- Mamzelle
- Missie
- Mopsy
- Mugsy
- Muffin
- Nibbles
- Lampchop
- Lolly
- Lovey
- Missy
- Mister
- Pachi/pachis (Armenian for kisses)
- Paws
- Peaches
- Peanut
- Peewee
- Petit chou (French for little cabbage)
- Pickles
- Pinky
- Pip
- Pippa
- Pippi
- Pompom
- Poo
- Pooch
- Pookie
- Poquita (o)
- Precious
- Pudding
- Puddles
- Pudgy
- Puffy
- Pumpkin
- Silky
- Smootch
- Snuggles
- Sonny
- Stinky
- Sugar
- Sweetpea
- Sweetie
- Taffy
- Tootsy
- Wiggles
- Yoyo
- Yumyum

Note: a endings for female; o endings for male

What a Concept

Like to see a little more peace and justice in the world? Looking for a name with lasting appeal, one that will stand the tests of time? These "concept" words are packed with message and meaning. Choose a word that has special significance for you. Every time you call your dog, you'll be reminded of your most cherished ideals.

O Bliss
O Blessing
O Brother
O Chance
O Charisma
O Charity
O Comfort
O Constance
O Courage
O Delight
O Democracy
O Destiny
O Duty
O Eternity
O Faith
O Fate
O Fortune
O Freedom

O Friend
O Future
O Grace
O Harmony
O Heaven
O Honor
O Hope
O Inspiration
O Journey
O Justice
O Liberty
O Luck
O Marvel
O Melody
O Mercy
O Merit
O Miracle
O Mystery

O Odyssey
O Patience
O Peace
O Pride
O Promise
O Providence
O Prudence
O Resolved
O Sister
O Trinity
O Truth
O Unique
O Secret
O Serenity
O Serendipity
O Smile
O Wisdom

Dogs of Mount Olympus

In ancient Egypt, cats were worshipped as gods. Hardly seems fair to the dogs, does it? To help even the score, why not pick a perfectly divine name for your new heavenly hound? Myths and legends from cultures around the world are full of interesting names for gods, goddesses, heroes, and heroines.

FEMALE	ORIGIN
⭕ Aphrodite	Greek goddess of love and beauty
⭕ Artemis	Greek goddess of the hunt and wilderness
⭕ Athena	Greek goddess of wisdom
⭕ Aurora	Roman goddess of the dawn
⭕ Brigid	Celtic goddess of inspiration and healing
⭕ Cassandra	Greek prophetess
⭕ Cassiopeia	Queen in Greek myth
⭕ Ceres	Roman goddess of the harvest
⭕ Electra	Figure in Greek myth
⭕ Eos	Greek goddess of the dawn
⭕ Freya	Norse fertility goddess
⭕ Frigg	Norse goddess of fertility and marriage
⭕ Io	Figure in Greek myth
⭕ Hera	Greek queen of the gods
⭕ Isis	Egyptian goddess
⭕ Juno	Roman queen of the gods
⭕ Kali	Hindu goddess of death and destruction
⭕ Luna	Roman goddess of the moon
⭕ Lalita	Hindu goddess of beauty
⭕ Maya	Hindu goddess of illusion and mystery
⭕ Minerva	Roman goddess of wisdom
⭕ Morrigen	Celtic goddess of war
⭕ Pandora	Figure in Greek myth
⭕ Pelé	Hawaiian volcano goddess
⭕ Persephone	Greek goddess of the harvest

○	Pinga	Inuit goddess of the hunt
○	Rhiannon	Celtic goddess of the moon
○	Pomona	Roman goddess of fruit trees
○	Saraswati	Hindu goddess of wisdom
○	Selene	Roman goddess of the moon
○	Soma	Hindu moon deity
○	Venus	Roman goddess of love
○	Vesta	Roman goddess of the hearth

MALE

○	Achilles	Greek hero
○	Adonis	Greek god
○	Ahti	Finnish god of lakes and streams
○	Aeneus	Greek hero
○	Apollo	God of poetry, music, and the sun
○	Ajax	Greek hero
○	Aries	Greek god of war
○	Atlas	Figure in Greek myth
○	Augustus	Roman emperor
○	Balder	Norse god of beauty and light
○	Bacchus	Roman god of wine
○	Cupid	Roman god of love
○	Ganesh	Hindu god of wisdom

○	Hercules	Greek god of strength
○	Hermes	Greek messenger of the gods
○	Hypnos	Roman god of sleep
○	Jupiter	Roman king of the gods
○	Loki	Trickster in Norse myth
○	Midas	King from Greek myth
○	Orpheus	Roman god of dreams
○	Nanook	Inuit master of bears
○	Neptune	Roman god of the sea
○	Odin	Norse king of gods
○	Orion	Figure from Greek myth
○	Pan	Mythical god of the forest
○	Perseus	Greek hero
○	Poseidon	Greek god of the seas
○	Remus	Figure from Roman myth
○	Romulus	Figure from Roman myth
○	Septimus	Roman emperor
○	Shiva	Hindu god of destruction
○	Thor	Norse god of thunder
○	Vayu	Hindu god of wind
○	Vulcan	Greek god of fire
○	Zephyr	Greek god of wind
○	Zeus	Greek king of gods

Double Dog Dare Ya

You're a risk taker, a rebel—you live on the
edge. So it's only fitting that when choosing
your dog's name, you pick something on the very fringe of
social acceptability. These names are a little risky, a little
dark. You may raise a few eyebrows calling one of these
names at the park, but that's just you being you.

- Attila
- Caligula
- Cerberus
- Chupacabra
- Chuckie
- Cruella
- Cujo
- Devil Dog
- Diablo
- Draco
- Dracula
- Fiend
- Freak
- Freddy
- Hannibal
- Harpy
- Hellhound
- It

- Jackal
- Jaws
- Killa
- Gangsta
- Lucifer
- Maleficence
- Medusa
- Mephisto
- Mordred
- Nemesis

- Psycho
- Scratch
- Skoll
- Terminator
- Wart
- Worm
- Viper
- Voldemort
- Zombie

Game Dogs

Put down the controller and step away from the game console—you and your dog are both going to need a little exercise. If you're having trouble taking your mind off your favorite video games, you can always name your dog after one of the characters. Video and computer game characters have some of the coolest, creative names anyone could ever dream up. Name your dog for a gutsy hero or even a dastardly villain—who could resist a toy fox terrier named Yuga the Destroyer? Or a German shepherd named Spirit of Cuteness?

- Aku Aku
- Ash
- Banjo Bear
- Blade
- Blanka
- Blaze
- Brock
- Bumper
- Cham Cham
- Chameleon
- Chocobo
- Cloudjin
- Conker
- Cortana
- Crash
- Crazy Redd
- Crunch
- Cyrax
- Dee Jay
- Deku
- Den
- Dingodile
- Doctor Nefarious Tropy
- Domino
- Earthquake
- Frogger
- Geki
- Goldeen
- Ebeneezer Von Clutch
- Gruntilda Winkybunion
- Heartless
- Humba Wumba
- Kazooie
- Kenshi
- Kirby
- Klungo
- Koopa
- Knuckles
- Khyber

- Lucy
  Fleetfoot
- Luigi
- Mingella
- Mondo
- Moogle
- Moppina
- Navi
- Nicotine
- Caffeine
- Nightwolf
- Nobody
- Pasadena
- O'Possum
- Pascal

- Pelly
- Pikachu
- Pinstripe
  Potoroo
- Pipsy
- Polar
- Princess Peach
- Princess
  Prin Prin
- Reptile
- Ripper Roo
- Ryu
- Sareena
- Scorpion
- Shinnok
- Sub-Zero
- Selphie
- Sonic
- Spirit of
  Cuteness

- Super Mario
- Swampy
- Tam Tam
- Tails
- Tawna
- Tiff
- Tiny Tiger
- Tiptup
- Tortimer
- Treeby
- Tuff
- Uka Uka
- Vega
- Wa-Wa
- Wanfu
- Willie Wumpa
  Cheeks
- Yuga the
  Destroyer
- Waddle Dee
- Wisp
- Zam
- Zem

The Classics

In the pantheon of dog names, these are the enduring classics. You may have had a dog with one of these names when you were a kid. Or you may just like the idea of your dog being part of a fine dog-naming tradition. These names may not be the most original, but they have a certain old-fashioned charm. You could say they're so out, they're in.

- Bandit
- Banjo
- Bingo
- Bitsy
- Blackie
- Bones
- Boots
- Boomer
- Buttons
- Brandy
- Brownie
- Bowser
- Buddy
- Buck
- Buster
- Butch
- Chief
- Cookie
- Copper
- Corky
- Cricket
- Duchess
- Duke
- Fido
- Fifi
- Ebony
- Ginger
- Gypsy
- Inky
- Jet
- Jinx
- Laddy
- Lassie
- Lucky
- Mickey
- Pal
- Patches
- Pepper
- Pooch
- Pretzel
- Rags
- Rambler
- Rascal
- Rex
- Roscoe
- Rover
- Ruffy
- Rusty

- ○ Sam
- ○ Scamp
- ○ Scooter
- ○ Scruffy
- ○ Scrappy
- ○ Skippy
- ○ Skipper
- ○ Scout
- ○ Snoopy
- ○ Smokey
- ○ Sparky
- ○ Spike
- ○ Spot
- ○ Sport
- ○ Shep
- ○ T-Bone
- ○ Tiger
- ○ Tiny
- ○ Troupe
- ○ Wags

Top Ten Dog Names in Japan

- ○ 1. Momo
- ○ 2. Koro
- ○ 3. Lucky
- ○ 4. Nana
- ○ 5. Hana
- ○ 6. Taro
- ○ 7. John
- ○ 8. Cocky
- ○ 9. Bell
- ○ 10. Chibi

Pick o' the Litter

#1

Still haven't found the perfect name? In that case, you might want to resort to what a lot of *other* people are naming *their* dogs. These lists—compiled from various sources in the U.S., Canada, the U.K., and Australia over the past three years—prove that as far as most folks are concerned, "keep it simple" is a motto to live by. Solid, sweet, and serviceable, these names have timeless appeal.

FEMALE

- ○ 1. Molly
- ○ 2. Maggie
- ○ 3. Daisy
- ○ 4. Sadie
- ○ 5. Princess
- ○ 6. Lady
- ○ 7. Lucy
- ○ 8. Chlöe
- ○ 9. Sophie
- ○ 10. Ginger
- ○ 11. Bailey
- ○ 12. Abby
- ○ 13. Bonnie
- ○ 14. Angel
- ○ 15. Sasha
- ○ 16. Roxy
- ○ 17. Zoë
- ○ 18. Brandy
- ○ 19. Annie
- ○ 20. Katie

MALE

- ○ 1. Max
- ○ 2. Buddy
- ○ 3. Jake
- ○ 4. Sam
- ○ 5. Bailey
- ○ 6. Rocky
- ○ 7. Jessie
- ○ 8. Cody
- ○ 9. Bear
- ○ 10. Buster
- ○ 11. Toby
- ○ 12. Lucky
- ○ 13. Charlie
- ○ 14. Oscar
- ○ 15. Harley
- ○ 16. Rusty
- ○ 17. Jack
- ○ 18. Sammy
- ○ 19. Murphy
- ○ 20. Sparky
- ○ 21. Shadow
- ○ 22. Barney

Index